GET READY
FOR THE
GOOD FIGHT

HUBERT E. THOMAS

GET READY
FOR THE
GOOD FIGHT

ARPress
45 Dan Road Suite 5
Canton MA 02021
Hotline: 1(888) 821-0229
Fax: 1(508) 545-7580

Ordering Information:
Quantity sales. Special discounts are available on quantity purchases by corporations, associations, and others. For details, contact the publisher at the address above.

Printed in the United States of America.

ISBN-13:	Softcover	979-8-89389-469-1
	eBook	979-8-89389-470-7

Library of Congress Control Number: 2024918275

Table of Contents

I am dedicating this book to my three wonderful children: Audrey P. Doukoure, Malcolm L. Thomas, and Josie P. Recine, all of which I am proud of. And to my seven grandchildren who I also love and adore: Christopher Thomas, Alexander Thomas, Matthew Thomas, Madeline Thomas, Mamadu Doukoure, Scheick Doukoure, and Omar Doukoure.

PREFACE

Dear readers, the following is a follow up or modification of my previous manuscript of my book, "Are You Ready For The Fight", which presents my reflections on the nature of the conflict in today's world; that, there is only really one good fight, and that is the fight not against fellow man but against "spiritual hosts of wickedness." From my experience, I believe that Christians have a duty to serve as good examples against these spiritual hosts. The many conflicts affecting people today are all the work of "the deceiver." It is how this evil one has decided to strike against God by going after His children, causing them to tear each other down, be it in petty arguments or outright war. It is through conflict that the deceiver shatters the interpersonal relationships among Christians.

"The God Fight" lays out a succinct action plan particularly for Christians to serve as good examples against the spirit of discord. I even use an analogy with boxing despite not wishing to promote the sport. I write this all just in the hope that more believers, and non-believers, will fight against being puppets of the deceiver. In this new book, I will build upon the nature of the fight, and the nature of God's earthly and heavenly children.

When Jesus was about to be arrested, Peter, in trying to defend Jesus, took out a sword and cut off the ears of one of the guards. Jesus then said to Him:

"Jesus answered, "**My kingdom is not of this world**. If **My kingdom** were **of this world**, **My** servants would fight, so that I should **not** be delivered to the Jews; but now **My kingdom is not** from here." John 18:36.

In other words, Peter did not understand the nature of his fight; therefore he was not ready for the fight. Jesus is now telling Peter that his fight was not of this world, but that God's kingdom soldiers fight differently. They fight the good fight. Jesus emphasizes that if His kingdom was of this world, he had myriads of angels that could free Him from the Romans. So, what is the nature of God's kingdom? How does the citizens of this kingdom behave while sojourning in this world? This is what this book is all about.

Jesus gives us a hint in His prayer to His father:

"Jesus spoke these words, lifted up His eyes to heaven, and said: "Father, the hour has come. Glorify Your Son, that Your Son also may glorify You, as You have given Him authority over all flesh, that He [a]should give eternal life to as many as You have given Him. And this is eternal life, that they may know You, the only true God, and Jesus Christ whom You have sent. I have glorified You on the earth. I have finished the work which You have given Me to do. And now, O Father, glorify Me together with Yourself, with the glory which I had with You before the world was. "I have [c]manifested Your name to the men whom You have given Me out of the world. They were Yours, You gave them to Me, and they have kept Your word. Now they have known that all things which You have given Me are from You. For I have given to them the words which You have given Me; and they have received *them,* and have known surely that I came forth from You; and they have believed that You sent Me. "I pray for them. I do not pray for the world but for those whom You have given Me, for they are Yours. And all Mine are Yours, and Yours are Mine, and I am glorified in them. Now I am no longer in the world, but these are in the world, and I come to You. Holy Father, keep through Your name those whom You have given Me, that they may be one as We *are.* While I was with them [e]in the world, I kept them in Your name. Those whom You gave Me I have kept; and none of them is lost except the son of perdition, that the Scripture might be fulfilled. But now I come to You, and these things I speak in the world, that they may have My joy fulfilled in themselves. I have given them Your word; and the world has hated them because they are not of the world, just as I am not of the world. ***I do not pray that You should take them out of***

the world, but that You should keep them from the evil one. [16] **They are not of the world, just as I am not of the world.** Sanctify[i] them by Your truth. Your word is truth. As You sent Me into the world, I also have sent them into the world. And for their sakes I sanctify Myself, that they also may be sanctified by the truth". John 17:1-20

For any training to be effective you need to practice and have an assessment. At the end of each chapter are some questions and things for you to do. Answer the questions honestly and to the best of your ability.

Use this workbook when you face the various challenges until the concepts or principles become part of your nature and character.

This book is intended to show how to fight the Christian warfare whether you are a Bible believer or not, these principles and lessons can benefit you. The purpose of this book is not to convert you, but to make a difference in your life.

I pray that this book will be a blessing to you. We are counseled in the Bible to "**Fight the good fight of the faith. Take hold of the eternal life to which you were called when you made your good confession in the presence of many witnesses." 1 Tim. 6:12 (NIV).**

Acknowledgments

These persons reviewed and made some suggestions, and thus have contributed to the success of this book. To them, I express my gratitude, and I feel compelled to highlight how I highly value their opinion and wisdom.

Gloria Trotman, PhD, CFLE
Malcolm L. Thomas, MA
Yvette de Thomas, MA

Introduction

The badge of Christianity is not an outward sign. The wearing of a cross or a crown does not indicate our persuasion, but it is that which reveals the union of man with God. By the power of His grace manifested in the transformation of character, the world is to be convinced that God has sent His Son as its Redeemer. No other influence that can surround the human soul has such power as the influence of an unselfish life. The strongest argument in favor of the Gospel is a loving and lovable Christian (Ellen White, *The Ministry of Healing*, 470.1).

> The Lord does not now work to bring many souls into the truth, because of the *church members who have never been converted*... What influence would these unconsecrated members have on new converts? Would they not make of any effect the God-given message which His people are to bear? (Ellen White, *Testimonies to the Church*, Vol. 6T. 370.3; italics mine)

The intent of this book is to deal with interpersonal relationship primarily among Christians and to remind them of the example they should be showing to others by their conduct. Non-Christians can also be benefited from the principles enunciated.

It also deals with one's behavior and attitude when facing physical and verbal challenges. I know that what will be presented in this book will be effective if followed for I currently am experiencing it and have proven it to be true. I have peace despite the many challenges that I face every day. This is why, when I am asked, "How are you today?" My response is always "Enchanted with life. My day is good every day because the day and challenges do not make me. I make the day."

In this book, I will present to you how to fight the Christian warfare using Christian principles. As you read, make it interactive. It will be more fun and effective.

Although, as Christians, we do not promote the activity in the boxing world yet we can learn some principles from their discipline. Therefore, I will include some boxing principles and illustrations from the boxing world to enhance the presentation along with some Bible references.

The Bible uses some illustrations from the physical athletic world to drive home points. Here are some:

1. The race of faith (Heb. 12:1).
2. Let us lay aside every weight.
3. Let us run with endurance the race that is set before us.
4. Boxing.
5. Fight the good fight (1 Tim. 6:12).
6. Thus, I fight not as one who beats the air (1 Cor. 9:26).

All Bible references are taken from the New King James Version (NKJV). Whether you are a Bible believer or not, these principles and lessons can benefit you.

The purpose of this book is not to convert you to any religion but to make a positive difference in your life and make it moreenjoyable.

I conducted a live presentation of the content of this book as a class. There were seventy-five people in attendance, and I did a survey at the end of the class in order to asses and evaluate the effectiveness. Below are the questions asked and the result in percentage.

1. Did anything in this presentation applied to you? 86.5 percent
2. Did you benefit from anything said?   92.5 percent
3. Will this presentation cause a change inyour life? 85.2 percent
4. Was the presentation clear?   92.8 percent
5. Do you now understand the nature of ourfight? 94.2 percent

I am also hoping that this book will also be read by those children who are being bullied and do not know how to cope with it.It makes me sad when I hear that students commit suicide because they could not cope with the bullying and often wonder why they did not have the confidence in their parents or any other adult to letthem know what they are going through. Chapter 6 will deal with this briefly.

For any training, to be effective, you need to practice. Go over the illustrations and answer the questions at the end of each chapter honestly and to the best of your ability.

Use this as a workbook when you face the various challenges until the concepts or principles become part of your nature and character.

I pray that this book will be a blessing to you. We are counseledin the Bible to "Fight the good fight of faith, lay hold on eternal lifeto which you were also called and have confessed the good confession in the presence of many witnesses" (1 Tim. 6:12).

Chapter 1

Fight the Good Fight of the Faith

There is a good fight, and there is a bad fight. The principle and issues involved apply to both Christians and non-Christians; both can benefit from the principles presented in this book.

One fight leads to eternal life and the other leads to hell. The first fight is the one implemented by the sincere Christians and by those non-Christian following biblical principles. The second is used by those not following biblical principles, including those who merely profess Christianity, but do not practice it inwardly nor outwardly.

There are many biblical principles that are so universal that are practiced by non-Christians and even nonreligious and nonspiritual people. Self-sacrifice, sharing, the golden rule, and honesty are some to name a few.

The Nature of the Fight

The first and primary issue is for us to understand the nature of the fight.

"For we do not wrestle against flesh and blood (*fellow human beings*), but against principalities, against powers, against the rulers of the darkness of this age, against spiritual *hosts* of wickedness in the heavenly *places*" (Eph. 6:12; italic mine).

In other words, though we contend daily with human elements, these are not primarily our opponents. Satan uses a lot of people as puppets. You see, he lost out to God in the beginning, and he now seeks vengeance.

"And the dragon was enraged with the woman, and he went to make war with the rest of her offspring, who keep the commandments of God and have the testimony of Jesus Christ" (Rev. 12:17).

Since he cannot really attack God, he tries to get back at Him by hurting His children whom God loves dearly.

During my school days, we used to play a trick on each other. Two friends would be talking and unknowing to either of them. I (the instigator) would take the hand of one of them (the puppet) and strike the other (the victim). The one being struck would believe that the person he was speaking to struck him. Because he did not see me, the real culprit, he would then strike back at the person he was speaking to, and despite any claims of innocence, a fight between them would ensue. I would stand back and laugh at the two victims of my little scheme.

What is really happening here? One individual is being used as a puppet, the other individual as a victim. The puppet is being used and does not know it. The victim does not see the instigator. He only sees and feels the effect of the puppet. He cannot be convinced that the puppet is innocent. He actually felt the blow, did not see anyone else around, and only saw the puppet, his attacker. No matter what you may say to the victim, you may not be able to convince him. Witnesses nearby saw what happened and know the truth yet they may not be able to convince the victim otherwise unless they try and try and bring solid proof.

The deceiver of the brethren (instigator) uses people as puppets to cause strife between them. One would lash back at the assumed instigator with verbal insults and even physical violence. Then Satan looks at them and laughs as if to say, "These two are fighting each other as enemies, not realizing that I am the instigator. They are also giving a bad example to the non-Christians since they call themselves *Christians*." It is of utmost importance that we understand the nature of our Christian fight since heaven or hell is at stake.

The

Instigator – puppet – victim – Helper in time of need

There are just one of two forces in the universe, directing the orchestra of humanity. Only one can direct an individual at any given time. One directs bringing disharmony and chaos, the other directs bringing peace and harmony.

Many members in this humanity orchestra believe that they are directing their own lives and ways of doing things, playing their own tune. Can you imagine overwhelming chaos that would happen in an orchestra if every member decided to play their own tune? The same would be if every single individual in this world directed his own life. Jeremiah knew this and said, "O Lord, I know the way of man *is* not in himself; *It is* not in man who walks to direct his own steps" (Jer. 10:23).

Many people in our world today are not aware of this, so they do not realize this. Since this is the greater truth and fact, we are advised, "In all your ways acknowledge Him, and He shall direct your paths" (Prov. 3:6).

Just as the trainer encourages his prize fighter at the break at the end of a round, reminding him of his training, the Bible also counsels us to "Lay hold on eternal life, to which you were also called and have confessed the good confession in the presence of many witnesses" (1 Tim. 6:15).

The Apostle Paul, who I consider a prize fighter in Christian principles, said this of his Christian *boxing* experience,

> I have fought the good fight, I have finished therace, I have kept the faith. Finally, there is laid up for me the crown of righteousness, which theLord, the righteous Judge, will give to me on thatDay, and not to me only but also to all who haveloved His appearing. (2 Tim. 4:7–12)

Please note the steps.

A. He fought the good fight.
B. He finished the race.
C. He kept the faith.
D. He has a crown of righteousness prepared for him.
E. The Lord will give it to him.
F. We can obtain one too if we also fight the good fight.

The common boxers use boxing gloves, short trousers, and boxing shoes to fight. They also use mouth gear. The amateur boxes add the use of head gear. What is the gear of the Christian boxer? The Armor of God.

> Finally, my brethren, be strong in the Lord and inthe power of His might. Put on the whole armorof God, that you may be able to stand against thewiles of the devil. For we do not wrestle against flesh and blood, but against principalities, againstpowers, against the rulers of the darkness of thisage, against spiritual *hosts* of wickedness in the heavenly *places*. Therefore, take up the whole armor of God, that you may be able to withstandin the evil day, and having done all, to stand. Stand therefore, having girded your waist with truth, having put on the breastplate of righteousness, and having shod your feet with the preparation ofthe gospel of peace; above all, taking the shield offaith with which

you will be able to quench all the fiery darts of the wicked one. And take the helmet of salvation, and the sword of the Spirit, which is the word of God; praying always with all prayer and supplication in the Spirit, being watchful to this end with all perseverance and supplication for all the saints. (Eph. 6:10–18)

Important issues to understand:

1. We don't use our physical strength, but God's.
2. We fight in God's power, not ours.
3. Our fight is more spiritual, mental than physical.
4. Our fight is centered around decisions.

The Environment of the Fight

We all live in a physical world, and this is what the majority see and understand. But there is more to this. When God made this world, it was His intention to populate it with people who would serve and obey Him and live by His rules. Sin has distorted God's plans to the extent that men thinks that everything is centered on them—how they feel and what they think to be correct. Men now act as if this is it as it is that this world is the ultimate environment. They do not realize that there are two coexisting worlds, namely, God's spiritual kingdom and a sin contaminated world. Here is what the Bible says about this.

1. There is a coexisting kingdom that is not of this world (John 18:36).

    Jesus answered, "My kingdom is not of this world. If my kingdom were of this world, my servants would fight so that I should not be delivered to the Jews; but now My kingdom is not from here."

2. Love not the world (1 John 2:15).

    Do not love the world or the things in the world. If anyone loves the world, the love of the Father is not in him.

3. The world hates you (John 15:19).

   If you were of the world, the world would love its own. Yet because you are not of the world, but I chose you out of the word, therefore the world hates you.

4. We are not to be taken out now (John 17:15).

   I do not pray that You take them out of the world, but that you should keep them from the evil one.

5. We have a divine purpose for still staying in the world now (Phil. 2:15).

   That you may become blameless and harmless, children of God without fault in the midst of a crooked and perverse generating, among who you shine as a light in the world.

6. People do not understand what they consider the Christian's strange behavior (1 Cor. 1:25).

   Because the foolishness of God is wiser than men, and the weakness of God is s stronger than men.

7. This world is now being used as a training ground (John 14:1–3).

   Let not your heart be troubled: you believe in God, believe also in Me. In my Father's house are many mansions; if it were not so, I would have told you. I go to prepare a place for you. And if I go to prepare a place for you, I will come again and receive you to myself; that where I am yours, may be theirs also.

8. The Christian's peace is different from what the world considers to be peace (John 14:27).

   Peace I leave with you, my peace I give you; not as the world gives do I give to you. Let not your heart be troubled, neither let it be afraid.

As stated before, it was not God's plan for us to live here on this earth under these stressful, uncertain, painful, and evil conditions. He is planning something better. But in the meanwhile, we must undergo some training and live here while He prepares a place for us with His original condition. He does not want us to be conformed to this world as it is now but to be transfused and to live our lives as if we are just transients or sojourners, waiting for the final transformation as we follow His guidelines for our conduct.

A person who is vacationing in another country does not have a lifestyle the one who permanently lives here. They do not set down their root; their activities are temporal.

This should be the attitude the people of God should assume. God has set out guidelines for the type of living and attitude we should assume, which the people of this world consider nonsense or foolishness.

Their lifestyle, speech, attitude, outlook, manner of deportment, amusement, etc., are different from those of this world. The good thing about these guidelines is that their principle is not only beneficial to Christians, but also to non-Christians. For example: I am a bookkeeper, not a racer. But if I practice all the exercises the racer does to keep in shape, it would be profitable for me.

I do not have to believe in racing, but if I see where the lifestyle they adopt in eating, exercising, sleeting, etc., would be beneficial to me. I would do them even if I do not race. My friends may not agree with me. They may think I am crazy, weird, and wasting my time, but I would not care what they may think of me because I would be getting the benefits, and that is enough for me. In this fashion, though you may not be a Christian, these Christians principle could be of great benefit to you.

Chapter 2

What Is Your Goal?

Except when purposely intend to lose a fight, every boxer's aim is to win. He sets goals he wants to achieve and marks out strategies he will use to win. The boxer is alert to the strategies his opponent may use to defeat him. Not only does he train to win the fight, but he also implements his training to the best of his ability.

You need to set goals beforehand as to what you want to achieve and how you want your life to be, and then work toward realizing those goals, not allowing anyone or anything to deter or defeat you.

Why set goals? The difference between who or what you say you are and who or what you really are is mostly in your head. Your mental commitment is the key for your reaching your goals. You may call yourself whatever you want to or say whatever you want to of yourself, but you cannot be whatever you claim to be if you do not set out your plans and follow them.

Your goals, plans, or decisions should be made long before you encounter the challenges. You may not be able to plan exactly for every challenge specifically, but you can plan for every challenge in principle.

Daniel "purposed in his heart" long before he faced the challenge of the king's meal. He had prepared himself for anything he would face in the future that would be against his moral principles. Daniel did not make the decision at the table. He prepared and made the decision in principle long before that testing moment.

When I was a boy of seven years of age, I took the advantage of my mother not being at home. One day, I went to the store and bought a cigarette and a flask of whiskey to see for myself the value people placed on them. I did not find any value in either one of them, so from then, I decided not to drink or smoke.

There were subsequent temptations, but they did not influence me, in the least. I never tried or tasted coffee. Because of the information I had of it, I decided in my mind never to touch it. No person or circumstance can force or influence me to use any of those substances. My goal was not to use them because of the harm that threatened me.

If you begin exercising without having a goal in mind, it will be like getting into your car and just driving without knowing where you will end up. If from the beginning you did not set a destination, how would you know that you are going in the right direction?

Your mind is set in motion by your goals and allows your action to follow. Without the goals, when you reach the challenges, you are going to ask yourself, "Why should I put up with all of this?" Then it becomes easy to quit.

- On a separate sheet of paper, list your goals in life—both spiritual and temporal. Make them realistic and achievable.

1. Make some about attitude, physical activities, lifestyles, etc.

2. Now list what would prevent you from reaching them.

Chapter 3

Let&s Get Ready to Rumble

Jabbing—Milk in the Face

A jab is a speedy powered punch. It makes an excellent defense and helps knock the opponent off balance. They are not expecting it. It is also intended to occupy the opponent's mind so that you can throw some more powerful combinations likewhat Alejandro Eubanks, a good colleague of mine, did while he wasstudying at school.

Alejandro and I studied together in COVAC, a boarding schoolin Alajuela, Costa Rica. The school had a plan, where the student worked on campus, to help with their tuition. One of these projectswas to sell books door-to-door. Alejandro's goal was twofold: One, to sell enough books to get a scholarship to pay his entire tuition; two, hope that the purchaser of the books may be benefited from them, especially being pointed to Christ.

So Alejandro went to a certain door at a home in Alajuela, Costa Rica. I do not know if the lady in the house had a problem with someone who come to her house before Alejandro got there, but when Alejandro knocked on the door, the woman opened the door.She had a glass in her hands filled with milk. She then threw the entire glass of milk into his face. What would you have done? Please,give a true and sincere answer as to what you would have done. Noone is there for you to impress with a dressed-up answer.

What did Alejandro do? Or let us start first with what he couldhave done.

1. Curse or insult the lady for throwing the milk in his faceand damaging his clothing.
2. Call the police.
3. Demand that she pays for dry cleaning.
4. Sue her.

He did none of the above. He had set his goals, and none of those actions would have helped him achieve his goals. So whatdid he do? He jabbed her. She was thrown off balance; she was not expecting it. Jabbed her, how?

He used a Christian principle that maybe she was not expecting. He was not going to allow this incident to detract him from his goals. He was not caught by surprised because he expected that someday something like this could happen. What he was about to do would be something that, for the natural human, is unnatural, but by God's grace and his predetermination became natural. Can you guess?

With his tongue going in a circular fashion, he licked the milk that was all around his mouth and said to her, "This milk would havebeen better inside than outside."

Suddenly, they both began to laugh. She took him inside and cleaned off the milk. Then he threw some powerful combinations ashe presented his sales pitch. She bought some books. Something that she might not have done had he insulted her or if she was not interested in the books. He achieved his goals, and they both were happy.

No one should or can prevent you from achieving your goals. You are the only one preventing yourself from achieving them. No one can make a fool out of you; only you can do this to yourself. A person's reaction should not dictate a negative reaction from you. They are not in control, you are.

The Bible presents a very important point that many people do not realize nor they do not understand the real issue of what is at stake. Whether you believe this or not, it is the real issues. I will state it again for emphasis and reinforcement, "For our struggle is not against flesh and blood, (*Fellow human*) but against the rulers, against the authorities, against the powers of this dark world and against the *spiritual forces of evil* in the heavenly realms" (Eph. 6:12). At the risk of redundancy, I will summarize: The devil uses people as puppets to start controversy. When they fight and insult each other, he sits back and laughs at the two, fighting each other. Remember, I said that his goal is to get back at God for expelling him from heaven. So since he knows that God loves His children, the devil uses God's children to blame and get angry at God.

Remember your goals you set for your present and future life. Before you retaliate, ask yourself, "Will my action help me reach my goals?" The fight then is determined by you and not by the other person. Therefore, you cannot blame others for your actions. This does not mean that we should be fools or make people use us as a floor mat. It only means that we must act prudently with wisdom and how Christ would want us to react. If you do this, jour jabs would beeffective, and you will win your fight.

Test Questions:

1. If instead of milk, the lady threw something else, what would you do?

2. In what way would you be benefited from your decision?

3. Give some references when and how you can use a jab.

4. As you face current challenges, write down what they areand how you plan to address them.

Chapter 4

Recycling Trash

Footwork—Horse in the Pit

The boxer knows that his footwork is very important. I enjoyed seeing the footwork of Sugar Ray Leonard and Muhammad Ali. It is the pivot for all other punches and activities. Footwork gives mobility, strength, and stamina to the restof the body. It moves the boxer in graceful and effective ways, like horse in the pit.

A horse was running in an open field and fell into a pit where people disposed their food and other garbage. It was very deep, so he could not come out by himself. He could do one of thefollowing:

A. Curse the people who made the hole and keep throwing garbage on him every day.
B. Have a pity party.
C. Just give up hope and lie down to die.
D. Let the garbage cover him.

Instead of any of these, this is what the horse did:

A. He began doing his footwork.
B. As the garbage was being thrown on him, he would shakeit off.
C. From the garbage, he would select things that were edible. This way, he was kept nourished and strong.
D. He walked around and got his exercise that strengthened his muscles and also made the ground under him solid. Eventually, the ground under him rose up to the level of the field. He was very strong and alive and ran away to a happy life.

Don't let others use you as their garbage pit or truck. This worldis so full of people carrying around garbage, looking for place to dump them, not caring how or where they dump them.

People are going to throw their garbage on you. They are goingto use you as their smelly garbage truck. This is when your footworkcomes into play. You can choose to

A. curse the people who threw their trash on you or have a pity party.

What good would this do you if you curse or have a pity party? Who cares? Or you could just give up, don't doanything, and let the garbage cover you. Then wither away with ulcers. You would be unwise to take this route.

A. do like the horse.
   b. Shake the garbage off you and just trample it under your feet.
   c. Analyze the criticism, insults, and garbage thrown on you first before taking an action. There may be some truth in them that you overlooked. Learn from them and be a better person if there is truth in the comments. Trample the bad under your foot. You see, this will make you a better and stronger person.

Another application of the footwork is the following:

Some people may think they are giving you what seems to be garbage to them when it could be something beneficial to you. Example: Once I saw piece of furniture that was being disposed of as garbage. It was shabby, and apparently, it was of no use to the original owner. Someone picked it up and was selling it for $25. They saw someone's garbage as a potential profit-making venture. I saw it, bought it, and what someone saw as garbage, I saw as a potential gem.

I took it home, took off the doors, sanded it smoothly, stained it, put gloss on it. What has someone's apparent garbage become a lovely dish china cabinet with a $300 value. See attached photo.

This happened in 2000, and we still have it. This is how it looks in 2019. Like the milk, some good things are thrown the wrong way.

Joseph told his brother, "You meant me evil, but God turned it into good." From being sold as a slave, being placed in jail, it resulted in his being a prime minister and helping a lot of people. What if he had become bitter and given up? People, all the time, recycle garbage into something good and useful.

If possible, find out why that person threw that garbage on you. Maybe you gave them a reason, maybe it could be some misunderstanding or misinterpretation, or maybe they are just evil and vindictive. Do some brainstorming as to how you can turn this into something positive and beneficial to you and others.

Whatever the reason may be, no one's garbage should be your garbage. Don't let them use you as their garbage truck. They dispose of it, and you are carrying it around. Shame, shame, shame on you.

So be nourished and strengthened by the good it may produce, then trample the trashy part under your feet. Do your footwork as a good boxer. Eventually, you will be able to move around and will rise to such a high level in your life that criticisms, insults, and garbage will not give you ulcers. You will not be offended by people's stupidity or insensitiveness.

1. Think of some previous experiences you might have had that could be like what was mentioned above. In what way were you benefited from your decision?
2. Give some references when and how you can use some footwork.
3. How will you turn it into something positive or beneficial to you?

Chapter 5

Enjoying a Trip to the Zoo

This Is Where You Use the "Duck"

When the opponent delivers a punch, the skillful boxer should be able to gracefully duck, thus, avoid a hit. The opponent's fist will go above you; you spring back, ready to deliver your blow.

Some people can be insulting and cloying. Some enjoy giving you a hard time. What can or should you do about this? Duck or goto the zoo.

Have you ever been to a zoo? What do people do in the zoo? I am sure to be entertained by the animals there. No matter what antics the animals come up with, you are not annoyed but entertained.

Someone has said that whenever someone tries to make your life difficult or annoy you, imagine you are in a zoo. This is where you use the duck as a boxer. Let their insults and antics pass over you.

Try to picture them as one of the animals, entertaining you with their antics, actions, attitudes, etc. Something like "He acts like a donkey," "Look at that snake," "What a beautiful parrot," "Boy, that is a stinking skunk." Get the picture? Quite funny, don't you think so?

So instead of being annoyed, you are being entertained. Then they, seeing you smiling (dance on the rope or Ali's rope-a-dope), will be wondering why they cannot hit you and why you are smiling, and they will get annoyed. There is your revenge. And you just laugh at the entertainers. You avoid getting ulcers. Dance on the rope like

Muhammad Ali. And as we use to say as kids, "Sticks and stones may break my bones, but words cannot hurt me."

The nations of today are developing people who are so easily offended. If you are called by any other name that is not your name, would you respond? If you are called an elephant, would you respond? Are you an elephant?

If someone calls me an elephant, I would think that person is crazy and imbecilic. How could they look at this wonderful specimen God made of me and call me an elephant? They need my prayers and sympathy, not my angry reaction. Why would I lose sleep orget ulcers over whatever some nincompoops say to me or about me while they go home and have a good meal and sleep? I am not even annoyed if they call me the *N* word. What does that mean? What do they mean? How does that affect me? How does that change me? Get the point?

If a person does not touch me, they cannot do or say anything that would get me annoyed. As we say in Spanish, "*Diga lo que le dala gana* (Say whatever you wish to say)." *It does not bother me. No one is that good or important to get me annoyed.* As someone said, "You can call me anything, but do not call me late for dinner."

Here is another instant where you go to the zoo. It is called forgiveness.

Forgiveness benefits the forgiver more than the forgiven one. Here is why.

When you do not forgive and *forget*, you are keeping that *acid* in your system. It is said that "Acid not only destroys the item that is thrown on but also that which contains it." When you keep that anger, resentful, unforgiven spirit in you, it affects you spiritually, physically, and mentally. Not forgiven does nothing to the person who did you wrong. It does not change them, it does not hurt them; it affects you. So there is no real revenge. They would live their life as if nothing happened (especially if they do not have a conscience). They would eat, be merry, and you are the one getting the ulcers.

I remember when I was nine years of age. We lived in a tenement building. Our neighbor Silvia, had a girl name Betty about two years younger than me. She was wild. They also had a young man about my age who they adopted as one of their family who visited them frequently but did not live there.

One day, Betty built a little tent outside of their apartment.She and Peter played in it. I did not go in but only curiously looked inside to see what she had in it. I did not know what Peter or anyoneelse did to her, but her mother discovered she had some scratch or bruise to her private part. She told her mother that I did it to her.

Lilian, Betty's aunt, told this to my mother. My mother asked me about it, and I told her that I did not know what she was talkingabout that I did not do anything and did not touch Betty. After several minutes of drilling, I repeated the same thing, insisting that I hadnothing to do with it. Lilian was condemning me. My mother did not believe me, so my mother called my cousin, Roy, and between them both. I got the worse whipping I ever had in my entire life.

I was very angry with my mother, my cousin Roy, Lilian, and especially Betty. If I had a chance, I would have ripped her to pieces. This anger lasted several years and bothered me until I finally let it go. I forgave them.

In 1962, when my grandmother passed away, I attended her funeral in Brooklyn, New York. On the Sabbath, I was there. I attended the Mount Olive Seventh-day Adventist Church. I met a good friend of mine who was the choir director. His name was Wilfred Moncrief. He asked me if I knew the song the choir was to sing that day, and if I would be willing to sing a duet with one of thechoir members. I said yes, I would be willing. Guess who was the choir member? Yes, it was Betty. We sang a wonderfully together. Up to this day, I have not told her about how I felt about the incident and how it had affected me.

As far as I am concern, it was forgiven and forgotten. As of thetime of the writing of this book, Peter is blind, and Betty has dementia or Alzheimer's and is now dead. As for me, I am enjoying life andthe best of health. God is in control I have no acid in my system.

The lesson is this: There is no doubt that people may do you wrong; there is no doubt that you may be hurt. But do not carry around this acid. Do not carry around this garbage. It will affect you. Furthermore, God say that we are not forgiven if we do not forgive.

1. Have you previously responded to insults? Did you benefit from your decision?
2. Give some references when and how you can use the duck and rope-a-dope.
3. Have you been hurt or wrongly accused?
4. How did you deal with it?
5. Are you still carrying around the garbage or acid?
6. If yes, how is this currently affecting your life? Is it worth it?

Chapter 6

Are You a Church?

Never Throw a Fight

The boxer with integrity will never throw a fight. He will not intentionally lose the fight of his own violation nor for any bribe or any pressure. His character will not allow him to do so, like the boy who said he was a church.

Roy was the best-behaved student in his class. As a matter of fact, the best in the entire school. When all the other students were being mischievous, he was not. He did his homework, was attentive in class, did not lie, and was very courteous. He never got into fights but always seemed to avoid them. He was not even annoyed by the school's bullies, who tried to make his life miserable.

When his teacher asked him why he was so good, he responded, "I am a church."

The teacher did not quite understand what he said, so she asked him, "What do you mean by that?"

He explained. "The Bible tells me that my body is the temple of the living God, so I must be a church and should act and behave like one."

Why do you behave as you do? How your peers or other pressure affects you?

There are lots of bullies that try to interrupt your peace. They are insecure and try to elevate themselves by putting you down. Remember this: they are below you and are trying to bring you down to their level. You're the most precious person in the sight of God. So no matter how others try to belittle you, it is only words; they need your prayers.

What work do you currently do? Are you being paid well? How much do you think they should pay you for your work that you would consider to be the right wages? Who do you work for? Do you work to satisfy that person?

I don't know about you, but I work to please God first, then myself. Next, I work for my employer. I do not primarily work for my employer; however, they reap the benefit of my working for God and myself and give me wages for it.

No one can put a correct value or tag on my work. It represents me. It tells what type of a person I am. It shows my character. I do the same supervised or unsupervised. I do not need supervision. If I cheat, I am cheating God and myself. Then I get the wages for it. Whatever I do, I do the best I can. Presently, I am an internal auditor. I enjoy my work. I do more than what is expected of me. I am being paid to do my hobby.

You must stand for principles and let them represent you. Do things not because of others or what they say you should do but because of the God-given principles you have set up for yourself. Daniel purposed in his heart that he would not defile himself with the king's meal. It was not dependent on the king or his meal. It was all about Daniel's character.

No one determines your character, but you. Danial did not wait until he came to that road to make his decision; he made it long ago. It was imbedded in him. He could not help it. It was his nature, his character.

The parable is told of a scorpion that wanted to cross over a river to get to the other side. He saw a turtle and asked the turtle to take him across on his back. The turtle refused, stating that, if he took the scorpion on his back. across the river sometime while crossing on his back that the scorpion would sting him, and both would die. The scorpion said he would not do that since he valued his life. The turtle was convinced, so he took him on his back to take him across to the other side.

During the journey, the scorpion stung the turtle. While sinking in agony to his death, the turtle cried out, "I thought you said you were not going to sting me?"

To which the scorpion responded, "I did not want to, but it is my nature to sting."

Just as it was the scorpion's nature to sting, though it meant his death, your nature should be to do your best and what is right.

By practicing the principles, I enunciated, it will become your nature to respond positively with the principles you set for yourself, and they will become part of your personality. You will not let people's bad attitude cause you to be like them. I have proven this to be so. You must realize beforehand who you are and what you stand for and don't care if others may be offended by your true principles. Many people today put the wrong value on issues.

The story is told about some boys who decided to do a prank on a neighborhood store. The store was having a weekend sale on some of its items. The manager placed low special Price tags on some of the items for sale. He also had regular price tags on those not included in the sale. The boys broke into the store and rearranged some of the tags. On the expensive items not for sale, they placed low sales price tags. On the cheap sales items, they put expensive sales tags. It was a mess when the store was open for sale, and the people came in to buy. This present world is a mess. Values are overstated at times and understated at other times. There are those who would like to impose their rotten values on you. But remember, you are a "church." Don't throw your fight.

1. The boy said he was a church, what are you? What do you stand for?
2. What will you now do when you are being bullied?

Chapter 7

You Can Only Give What You Have

The Upper Cut—Not Expecting It

I t comes up unexpectedly. It goes to the stomach or to the chin, throws the opponent off balance, not what they were exposing.

Tanya was a true and wonderful Christian woman who hadone big problem: her neighbor, Rose, who did everything to make Tanya's life miserable.

One day, Rose cleaned her house thoroughly and put some of the rubbish into a nicely wrapped box with a beautiful ribbon. She took it over to Tanya's house and gave it to her. Tanya was very surprised yet happy. *Is it that Rose was converted and has changed*? She could not contain this good news, so she called her husband and two children to witness the opening of this wonderful gift from Rose. When they opened the box, they all saw the rubbish. What would you have done if this happened to you?

Well, Tanya got a larger box along with some gift paper that was more beautiful and more wonderful gift wrapper. She went to the market and bought some nice, sweet smelling, luscious, and greatfruits, then put them into the box. She wrapped it nicely and put onthe ribbon but left the top open so that Rose would see it was not anyrubbish in it. She took this over to Rose and gave it to her, saying, "Everyone gives what she can afford to give."

ToonClips.com   #422   service@toonclips.com

There are several very important things to consider.

1. No one can make you do anything you do not want to do.
2. No one can make you be what you are not.
3. No one's action should be the deterring factor for youraction or reaction.
4. You can only give what you have.

Some people often say, "He or she made me do it." That is unadulterated sheer nonsense. You do it because that is who and what you are. It is just a cop-out. The other person had nothing to do with it, except to serve as a trigger for your actions.

Sam was a thief. He often stole things. One day, the pastor called Sam aside and asked him why he stole things.

"I do not know, Pastor," he replied. "I want to stop, but I cannot."

The pastor thought that this was a moment to be taken advantage of and point Sam to Christ.

He told Sam, "Jesus is willing to help you. The next time you are tempted to steal, just say, 'Get behind me, Satan,' and this wouldhelp."

www.clipartof.com · 1299491

A few weeks later, the pastor saw Sam stealing at a stall of apples. The pastor stood there, looking at Sam. Sam stood there, looking atthe apples but did not do anything.

The pastor then said to himself, "Sam won the victory." Just then, he saw Sam take an apple and ran away with it. He followed Sam, caught up with him, and asked, "Did I not tell you that stealingis wrong, and that you should have said to Satan get behind me?"

Sam replied, "Yes, Pastor, I did. I told Satan to get behind me. It worked for a while, but Satan got behind me and pushed me intothose apples, so I was forced to take one."

Often we wrongly blame Satan and others for our actions.

If someone curses or insults you and you return the insults using bad and offensive language, it is not their fault. It is just who or what you are inside. You cannot give garbage if you do not have any garbage. Note the following points:

1. *Wickedness proceeds from the wicked.*

> David also arose afterward, went out of the cave, and called out to Saul, saying, "My Lord, the king!" And when Saul looked behind him, David stooped with his face to the earth, and bowed down. And David said to Saul: "Why do you listen to the words of men who say, 'Indeed David seeks your harm?' Look, this day your eyes have seen that the lord delivered you today into my hand in the cave, and *someone urged me to kill you. But my eye spared you, and I said, 'I will not stretch out my hand against my lord, for he is the lord's anointed.'* Moreover, my father, see! Yes, see the corner of your robe in my hand! For in that I cut off the corner of your robe, and did not kill you, *know and see that there is neither evil nor rebellion in my hand,* and I have not sinned against you. Yet you hunt my life to take it. Let the lord judge between you and me, and let the lord avenge me on you. But my hand shall not be against you. As the proverb of the ancients says, 'Wickedness proceeds from the wicked.' But my hand shall not be against you. (1 Sam. 24:8–13; italic mine)

At that time, it was not part of David's character to kill, so killing could not come out of him. He did not have that to give.

2. *A good tree cannot bear bad fruit.*

Even so, every good tree bears good fruit, but a bad tree bears bad fruit. A good tree cannot bear bad fruit, nor *can* a bad tree bear good fruit (Matt. 7:17–18).[1]

---

[1] https://www.biblegateway.com/passage/?search=Matthew+7:17&version=NKJV.

3. *A good man out of the good treasure of his heart brings forth good.*

> A good man out of the good treasure of his heart brings forth good; and an evil man out of the evil treasure of his heart brings forth evil. For out of the abundance of the heart his mouth speaks (Luke 6:45; Matt. 12:35).[2]

4. *Your response condemns or justifies you.*

> And He said, "What comes out of a man that defiles a man" (Mark 7:20).[3]

Let us consider four basic reasons why people would give you garbage and then analyze the possible reactions.

1. Intended as humor.
   a. The person has the confidence that you can take a moment of humor.
   a. They have bad sense of humor.
2. It is their nature.
3. They have willful malice.
4. They are ignorant of the fact that it is garbage.

So are you are going to allow these people to sink you to their level? You dare not.

Has anyone given you their garbage? What was your reaction or should have been?

---

[2] https://www.biblegateway.compassage/?search=Matthew+12:35&version=NKJV.

[3] https://www.biblegateway.com/passage/?search=Mark+7:20&version=NKJV.

Chapter 8

Can't Move It, So I Will Build Around It

I n my estimate, there are just two types of challenges: The first you can do something to change the outcome or circumstance.

The second, you may not be able to do anything to change the outcome or circumstance. This could be a physical challenge.

Each person is different in how they face these. I cannot determine how you will react, but I can suggest and say how I would. If I can make a change, I will. If I cannot make a change, I am not going to fret, worry, and get ulcers. Whatever I cannot change, I would look for a way around it and be happy.

Example: Let us say I come across a steel wall that is unmovable. I am not going to hit my head against it; I am not going to cry, "Oh, this wall is in my way. I am so frustrated. Who put this wall here anyway?" This will not get me anywhere but will make things worse for me. Instead, I will find a way to go over, around, or under it. In finding the various possible ways to overcome it, I will be amused and activate my brain for having fun. In other words, my seeking an alternate solution will result in a blessing to me.

In high school, social studies was the only subject I get *D*s or *F*s. I did not like it. It was difficult for me. But math was easy. I always got *A*s. I even came first place in the school's math contest.

One day, I said to myself, "Hubert, you can do better than that. Why not try to get *A* in this subject?" So I got started on a revolutionary study program with this subject. The day came for me to put my efforts to a test; there was going to be an important social studies test.

The day of the test, we all sat down at our desks. The teacher, Profesora Perez, gave out the test papers facedown, and we waited for her command to start the test. When it was time to start, I turned over my paper and gave it an overall glance; it looked so easy. (Of course, anything is easy if you are well prepared for it.) I finished mine in record time and was the first to get up and give in my papers. Profesora Perez was shocked. Of all the students, Hubert was the first to finish. I smiled and left the classroom. The rest of the students came out much later. Some stayed to the bell.

The custom was to grade the test, give it back to the students the next day, call the name from the highest scores to the lowest, then go over the answers. I was so sure that my name would be called out first that I would get an *A* that even if there were other with *A*s, mine would be better than theirs. So here went this thrilling soapbox opera experience.

She called out the first A, but it was not mine. I said, "Hubert, don't be foolish. And *A* is an *A*." But when she called out all the As, my name was not there. She called all the *B*s; my name was not among them. The *C*s and *D*s, still my name not mentioned. Then a miracle happened when she called the *F*s. Hubert's name was called. She gave me my paper with a big *F*. She then proceeded to give the correct answers. Well, what do you know? My answers were all correct 100 percent. I felt glad. The teacher made a big mistake. I took it to her and showed her that all my answers were correct.

She said, "Thomas, look at your grammar. You got an *A* in social studies answers but an *F* in grammar."

I said, "You are a social studies professor, not a grammar professor."

She then responded, "In my classroom, I correct everything— social studies, math, grammar, etc.,"

Of course, I argued with her, but nothing changed. She was one of those unmovable wall or circumstance that I could not change. Did I cry, pout, shout, get a tantrum, or worry myself? Did I curse the professor? No, from then and onward, I took grammar seriously and did well in it up to this day.

As stated before, you change things and circumstances that are within your power and ability to change. What you cannot change find a way to go around it, and that would make you happy. And you know something sometimes these things could result in a blessing to you.

Take, for instance, the story in the Bible of Balaam and his donkey. For this illustration, let us think of the donkey as a challenge.

You see, God allows the challenges to come to us to make us Better persons, to refine us. They can come in the form of a person or circumstances. If we do not master the situation at hand, the subsequent ones will be more difficult.

Let me first explain the plot. Balaam disobeyed a command from God and was on his way to carry out his act of disobedience. There was an angel with a sword ready to destroy him. But God, in His love, used the donkey to try to deter him from carrying out his act of disobedience.

So here goes:

One day, Balaam was riding on his donkey on a mission that annoyed God. God was angry with him but tried to deter him from carrying out his act of disobedience. As he was going, there was an angel with a sword ready to kill him. He did not see the angel, but the donkey did. So the donkey went off in on a sideroad. Balaam was angry and struck the donkey to get him back on the pathway.

Lesson One

There are times God allows certain challenges to come our way to test us or refine us or guild up our character. We may not see it that way nor understand it. We do not need to understand but must be sure that we are really serving Him sincerely and understand that He cares for us and knows why and what He is doing. He makes Himself responsible for the outcome. Just trust Him and praise Him. Never get frustrated nor curse or beat the challenge, like Balaam did. The donkey had a reason for going in another direction.

The donkey continued. So the angel with the sword stood in a narrow path this time where there were walls on each side, ready to kill. The donkey saw the angel, and then it crushed Balaam's foot against the wall, hoping this would stop him from going forward for going in another path was not enough, so crushing his foot may succeed. But Balaam got angrier and struck the donkey again.

Lesson Two

When we fail to overcome or conquer a challenge, it will keep coming back, and it gets worse or harder. Instead of trying to analyze the situation, Balaam got angrier and continued to strike the donkey. This got him nowhere for the donkey continued. Then the angel of the lord went further and stood in a narrow place where there *was* no way to turn either to the right hand or to the left. And when the donkey saw the angel of the lord, she laid down under Balaam, so Balaam's anger was aroused, and he struck the donkey with his staff. Notice what the donkey did: going in another path that did not work, making things harder by crushing his foot against the wall that did not work. So he put on extreme measure. He just stopped, laid down, and did not advance. That did not work either. He was about to go to his death, then God, in His love intervened, he opened his eyes. Some people may not have been that fortunate.

Lesson Three

Failure to overcome the previous challenges will ultimately lead you to a dead end. It will be more difficult for you to overcome the future challenges. Your character will be of such that you get angrier and do things or act in way that may be detrimental to you. It may end very disastrous for you. But because of His love, God may cause your eyes to be open to the danger you are about to face in some strange or unexplainable fashion.

> Then the lord opened the mouth of the donkey, and she said to Balaam, "What have I done to you, that you have struck me these three times?" And Balaam said to the donkey, "Because you have abused me. I wish there were a sword in my hand, for now I would kill you!" So, the donkey said to Balaam, "*Am* I not your donkey on which you have ridden, ever since *I became* yours, to this day? Was I ever disposed to do this to you?" And he said, "No." Then the lord opened Balaam's eyes, and he saw the Angel of the lord standing in the way with His drawn sword in His hand; and he bowed his head and fell flat on his face. And the Angel of the lord said to him, "Why have you struck your donkey these three times? Behold, I

have come out to stand against you, because *your* way is perverse before Me. Thedonkey saw Me and turned aside from Me thesethree times. If she had not turned aside from Me,surely, I would also have killed you by now, andlet her live." (Num. 22:28–33)

Lesson Four

Do not let people or circumstances or challenges control you. Study them, analyze them, and see how they can be recycled into something beneficial to you. You will always have the option of making the right decision. Don't allow these to make you their slaves. Here is good advice from the Bible, "For by whom a person is overcome, by him also he is brought into bondage" (2 Peter 2:19).

Chapter 9

Make Sure Your Facts Are Confirmed

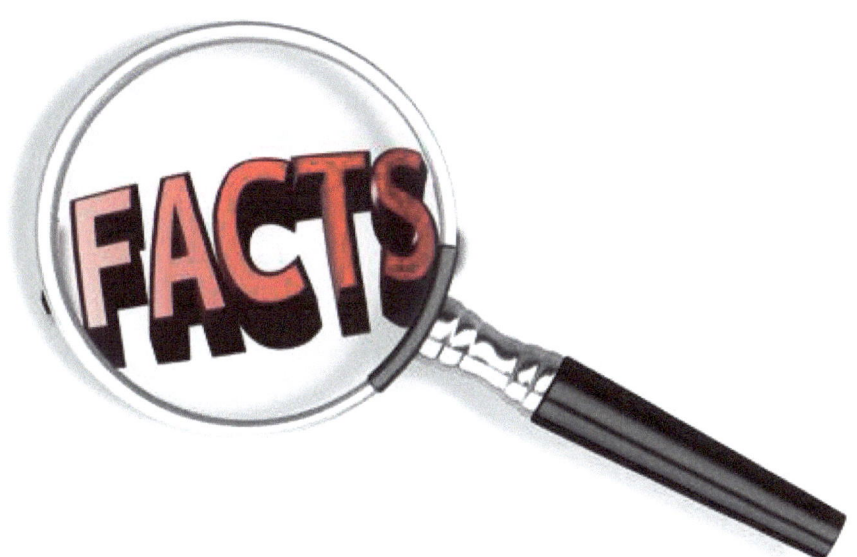

Listen to this wise advice from the Bible, "Examine yourselves *as to* whether you are in the faith. Test yourselves. Do you not know yourselves that Jesus Christ is in you? Unless indeed you are disqualified" (2 Cor. 13:5).

And why do you look at the speck in your brother's eye, but do not perceive the plank in your own eye?

Or how can you say to your brother, "Brother, let me remove the speck that *is* in your eye," when you yourself do not see the plank that *is* in your own eye? Hypocrite! First remove the plank from your own eye, and then you will see clearly to remove the speck that is in your brother's eye. (Luke 6:41, 42)

To introduce and illustrate this point, I will present, to the best of my recollection, an incident I just learned of.

A certain preacher went into a barber shop to get his regular haircut. While in there, a young man with a hoodie entered the barber shop. As he entered, he was looking back on the outside several times. The preacher got suspicious and thought that this young man was a thug and may had the intention of robbing and was looking back outside for his other companions. The barber also got suspicious and got out his gun.

Wisely, the preacher approached the young man and asked, "Why are you looking outside so often?"

To which he replied, "I am looking for my mom. She brought me here."

Here are some assumable facts, but are they factual?

1. Some people, when they go to rob, may have others helping with the lookout and escape vehicle. They would be looking back to be assured that the help is still there.
2. Most thugs use hoodies when committing a crime.
3. The barber might have had the experience of being robed; the preacher too.
4. They had reasonable reasons to be suspicious and to be on guard.

What was the truth? He was looking for his mother who brought him to the barber for a haircut. The mother eventually came to pick him up and pay for the haircut.

There is nothing wrong in being cautious when you do not have all the facts. But do not assume that you are correct until you are able to ascertain the truth of a matter or of a person. You must be careful of how you judge a person or circumstance or how they mayappear to be. You may not know what a person is going though whythey act how they do or say what they say. It may not be about you but about some trauma they have or are going through.

You may pass a person on the street or in church and say good morning to them, and they just ignore you. You cannot assume that they are rude to you, then you get angry with them and speak ill of their manners. You may not know why certain people appear bitter all the time. It could be that, if you get to really know the person, they are the sweetest person ever, but due to some circumstance in their lives or even their natural facial looks, they appear bitter.

Look not to a person or some circumstances by your own experience or how you may biasedly look at things. For example: Let us suppose that I select three groups of people. I give group A clear-colored pair of glasses; group B a green-tinted pair of glasses; group C a red-tinted pair of glasses. I then put the three groups in front ofa white wall and ask them to tell me the color of the wall they are seeing.

Group A group would say, "We see a white wall."

Group B would say, "We see a green wall."

Group C would say, "We see a red wall."

Would they be all correct as to what they saw under their specific conditions? Yes, of course, correct as to what they saw. But would they be all correct? No. Their answers would be subjected totheir programmed conditions.

In conclusion, let us make sure we do not judge people or circumstance by some preprogrammed condition of ours. Applying the principle of the text: "Examine yourselves *as to* whether you are in the *truth.*" (Truth is my application.) Test yourselves. (Your apparentfacts.) "Do you not know yourselves, unless indeed you are disqualified" (2 Cor. 13:5).

Consider also that there could be as beam in our eyes that is preventing us from seeing the truth about the person or circumstance.

Just like the lady who always complained to her friends and husbandthat her neighbor always washes her white clothes and hang them outto dry, but the clothes were always dirty. The husband got tired of hercomplaint and washed their window.

The next day, when she looked out of her window at the neighbor's clothesline, and she said, "So she finally got them real clean, and they look so superb."

The husband then said to his wife, "It is because I washed our window."

Readers, make sure your window is washed clean before to lookout at your neighbor on the other side.

Chapter 10

Be Wise

Tips from the life of Joseph

"A smart man profits from his mistakes, but a wise
man profits from the mistakes of others."
—**Berry Gordy**

If we want to know how any machinery or artifact operates at
its best, we go to the manual the manufacturer made for it. If we
want to know how we can function at our best, and maintain an
excellent inter personal relationship, we must go the Manual, God,

our Creator, made for us and gave us. It is the Bible. It does not matter if you believe this or not, it is a fact andthe unadulterated truth.

Jeremiah 10:23 NKJV states that:

"O Lord, I know the way of man *is* not in himself; *It is* not in man who walks to direct his ownsteps"

So, God gives us direct and indirect examples and stories as to how to succeed and be happy, in spite of circumstances, environment, dysfunctional family background, hereditary condition, past experiences, etc.

One of these Biblical example is found in the story of Joseph. I will now quote from lesson 6 and 7, "Finding Rest in Family Ties"and "Rest, Relationships, *and* Healing" from the The Seventh-day Adventist Lesson Study for July 31 to August 13, 2021. I will be adding some of my comments to it. I am using these particular lessons because they describes accurately how, in spite of existing conditions, we should make the decisions that would improve our lives and notallow others nor the conditions to make those decisions for us. It also describes and prescribe what should be our attitude towards those who have done us wrong, or are trying to sabotage our interpersonalrelationship. At the end of this chapter, which will be complimentedby the last chapter, if you truly and sincerely follow the instructions,you will be a new person; one who will be happy, peaceful and enjoylife to its fullest in spite of what you went through in the past, or willgo through now and in the future. You will be ready for the fight.

Joseph Background and Experience

Joseph was born in the bosom of a religious family, but his family was far from perfect (do perfect families even exist?). Everything he learned about God, thanks to his family, was thekey to making the right decisions in both tough and easy times.

This is the first step for us, learn about God and His direction for our lives

Joseph was spoiled, abandoned, humiliated, exalted, defamed. His life was in constant change. However, *the circumstances did not shape his destiny, but his decisions did.*

I reiterate and reemphasize: No one, nor circumstance can force you to do anything; you are the one, with the help of God, deciding how you proceed and the decision you make.

Dysfunction at Home-When your family is not perfect

Joseph came from a line of dysfunctional families.

Starting with his great-grandparents, Abraham and Sarah.

1. When Sarah realized that she was barren, she had convinced Abraham to go to her servant Hagar. As soon as Hagar was pregnant, the rivalry began. *Ishmael was born from Hagar and Isaac from Sarah.*
2. Ishmael and Isaac took the tension into their own families. Isaac made a point of favoring Esau, and Jacob spent his life trying to earn his father's love and respect.
3. Jacob was tricked into marrying two sisters who did not get along and competed with each other through a childbearing race, even enlisting their maids to bear Jacob's children.
4. Joseph's older brothers already had massacred all the males in the town of Shechem.
5. The oldest brother Reuben displayed dominance and defiance to his aging father by sleeping with Bilhah, (*his father's concubine*)
6. Joseph's brother Judah mistook his widowed daughter-in-law for a prostitute and ended up having twins with her.
7. Jacob added fuel to the fire of all this family tension by his obvious favoritism toward Joseph in giving him an expensive colorful coat.
8. If ever there was a dysfunctional family, the patriarch's family could have competed with it.

Choosing a New Direction-When you begin from scratch

Joseph must have been in pain

With this complicated relationship in his life and mind, with great anxiety with him as he travels to Egypt, where he is to be sold as a slave he should have been in pain. Are there some experiences in your life that would make you identify with this?

> "…Often in his father's tent he had listened to *the only tool he had to help him. It was to turn his thoughts to his father's God. In his childhood he had been taught to love and fear Him.* Now all these precious lessons came vividly before him. Joseph believed that the God of his fathers would be his God. *He then and there gave himself fully to the Lord, and he prayed that the Keeper of Israel would be with him in the land of his exile.*"
> — Ellen G. White, Patriarchs and Prophets, pp. 214 (italics supplied).

Joseph begins to find rest in his relationships by making a personal decision to follow God.

> **To find rest, we each must make a personal decision to follow God. Even if our ancestors were spiritual giants, this faith and spirituality aren't transmitted genetically.**

Finding True Self-Worth-When you are a nobody

Joseph is resold into a prominent household

Suddenly the young man was thrust into a strange new language and culture. But who was he now? A slave, someone who could be bought or sold at will. Look at how quickly his whole situation changed. Look at how quickly life seemed to have turned on him. Indeed, Joseph learns the lesson that we all have to learn. He did not complain or start the blaming game.

> *If we are dependent on others to tell us what we are worth, then we will be in for a rough ride and be horribly confused, because not everyone is going to appreciate who we are or what we are like. Instead, we need to find our self-worth in what God thinks of us—how God sees us— and not in the roles that we currently have.*

Joseph's self-esteem was not based on what others thought about him, but on his worth to God.

How does God look at you? God looks at each of us with glasses tinted with grace. He sees a potential, beauty, and talent that we can't even imagine. Ultimately, Jesus was prepared to die for us so that we could get the opportunity to become all we were created to be. Though showing us our sinfulness and the great price it cost to redeem us from it, the Cross also shows us our great worth and value to God. Regardless of what others think of us or even what we think about ourselves, God loves us and seeks to redeem us from not only the power of sins now but from the eternal death that they bring.

Doing Relationships God's Way-When your relationships are troublesome

Initially Joseph's story in Egypt takes a positive turn.

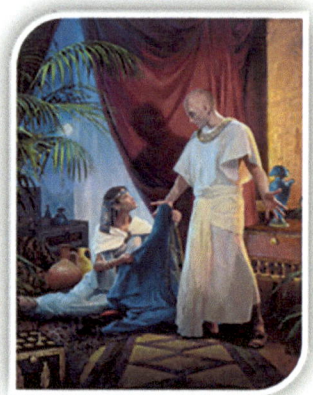 

Joseph has entrusted himself to God, and God blesses Joseph, who rises to heights he would not have imagined in Potiphar's household. Although Joseph seems to be getting along very well with Potiphar, and his relationships among the staff in the house and on the field seem to be smooth — trouble is brewing. Someone at home is restless Joseph has a problem with Potiphar's wife. Perhaps we should reformulate that: Potiphar's wife has a problem. She looks at others as "things" that can be manipulated and used. She wants to "use" Joseph.

Despite this wicked woman's insistence, Joseph does something seemingly counterproductive. He applies biblical principles to all relationships — in this case Potiphar's wife. Joseph realizes that he cannot control the choices of others. He decides, however, to live, love, and treat those around him in a way that will honor God. Joseph has learned to live in God's presence. This knowledge helped him resist temptation.

The Great Controversy, Up Close and PersonalWhen you are facing new challenge

Joseph suffers because of his principled decision.

Joseph is thrown in prison. Life on planet earth isn't fair. Good is not always rewarded, and evil is not always immediately punished. There is some good news though: Joseph can find rest, even in prison, because God is with him. In prison he could have meditated on the unfairness of his situation, withdrawn, and even given up on God. In prison, Joseph works with the real, not the ideal. He networks; he helps others, even though situations in prison were far from the ideal that he must have wished for.

In prison, Joseph is not above asking for help and making himself vulnerable. He asks for help from the cupbearer when he interprets his dream. Satan has a vested interest in using all our relationships—especially those closest to us—to his advantage in order to hurt and frustrate God's will for our lives. We can be thankful that we are not left to fight these battles on our own

Facing the Past-Has anything changed?

Eventually, things moved in the right direction for Joseph, big time. He not only gets out of prison, but he is made prime minister of Egypt after interpreting Pharaoh's dreams (Genesis 41). He is married and has two children of his own *(Gen. 41:50-52)*. The storehouses of Egypt are full, and the predicted famine has begun. And then, one day, Joseph's brothers turn up in Egypt Joseph had the power and could have taken his revenge on his brothers without having to justify himself. But, rather than revenge, Joseph is concerned about the members of his family at home. He is worried about his father. Was he still alive, or had a dysfunctional family become a family without a patriarch? And what about his brother Benjamin? As his father's delight and joy, Benjamin was now in the same position that Joseph had been. Had the brothers transferred their dangerous jealousy to Benjamin? Joseph is now in a position to look out for these vulnerable people in his family, and he does just that.

Practicing biblical principles in our relationships will not mean that we ever can or should accept abuse. Each one of us is precious in God's sight. Jesus paid the ultimate price on the cross for each one of us.

Setting the Stage-Have they repented?

Joseph has forgiven his brothers. We don't know exactly when Joseph forgave them, but it was obviously long before they showed up. Joseph probably would never have thrived in Egypt if he had not forgiven because, most likely, the anger and bitterness would have eaten away at his soul and damaged his relations with the Lord

Several studies of survivors of tragedy inflicted on them by others have highlighted the fact that for victims of the most horrible suffering, forgiveness was a key factor to find healing and to get their lives together again. Without forgiveness, we remain victims.

Forgiveness has more to do with ourselves than with the person or persons who have wronged us.

Even though Joseph has forgiven his brothers, he is not willing to let the family relationships pick up where he left them; that is, at the dry pit at Dothan. He has to see if anything has changed. All communication has been taking place through an interpreter, and so Joseph's brothers are unaware that he can understand them. Joseph hears his brothers' confession. The brothers had thought that by getting rid of Joseph, they would be free from his reporting to their father. They thought that they would not have to put up with his dreams or watch him revel in the role of being their father's favorite.But instead of finding rest, they have been plagued by a guilty conscience all these years. Their deed had led to restlessness and a paralyzing fear of God's retribution. Joseph actually feels sorry for their suffering. He weeps for them.

Joseph knows that the famine will still last several more years, and so he insists that they bring Benjamin back with them the next time they come to buy grain. He also keeps Simeon hostage. After seeing that Benjamin is still alive, he organizes a feast in which he obviously shows favoritism to Benjamin to see if the old patterns ofjealousy were still there. The brothers don't show any signs of beingjealous, but Joseph knows how cunning they can be. After all, they did deceive a whole town and he surely figures that they must have lied to their own father about his fate so, he devises one more majortest.

Forgive and Forget—Should I forgive them?

Forgiveness has been defined as the willingness to abandon one's right to resentment, condemnation, and revenge toward an offender or group who acts unjustly.

Dr. Marilyn Armour, a family therapist who worked withHolocaust survivors in order to find out what these survivors had done to make sense of what had happened to them, writes: "The whole idea of forgiveness is an intentional act by the victim. It's not something that just happens."

Forgiveness doesn't mean that there will be no consequences. Forgiveness doesn't mean letting an abuser continue abusive patterns. Forgiveness means, instead, that we turn our resentment and our desire for revenge over to God. If not, the anger, the bitterness, the resentment, and the hatred will make whatever that person or persons did to us even worse.

No question, one of the keys in learning to forgive is to understand what we have been forgiven in Christ. We have all sinned, not just against other people but against God, as well.

Every sin is, indeed, a sin against our Lord and Maker; and yet, in Jesus, we can claim total forgiveness for all those sins, not because we deserve it — we don't — but only because of God's grace toward us. Once we can grasp that sacred truth, once we can make this forgiveness our own, once we can experience for ourselves the reality of God's forgiveness, we can begin to let go and forgive others. We forgive not because others deserve it but because it's what we have received from God and what we need ourselves. And besides, how often do we deserve forgiveness, as well?

As we saw, too, Joseph offered a second chance for the family relations. No grudges here; no falling back to things that happened in the past. It is almost impossible to begin again in a family when we have each become experts at learning how best to hurt each other. But that's not how Joseph reacts. It seems that he wants to put the past behind them and to move ahead with love and acceptance. Had Joseph a different attitude, this story would have had a different ending, one not so happy.

Making It Practical - Who should take the first step?

1. In order to forgive, I must admit that I have been hurt. This can be hard to do, as we are sometimes more inclined to try to bury our feelings rather than work through them.

2. Acknowledging unchristian feelings of resentment and even anger before God is fine. We see this often expressed in the Psalms. I can feel free to tell God that I didn't like what happened or how I was treated and that it makes me sad or angry or both.

3. In Joseph's story, we see him crying as he sees his brothers again and relives some of the feelings of his past.

4. Jesus didn't wait for us to ask for forgiveness first. We do not have to wait for our offender to ask for forgiveness. We can forgive others without having them accept our forgiveness.

5. Forgiveness, like love, begins with a choice rather than a feeling. We can make the choice to forgive, even if our emotions may not agree with this decision. God knows that in our own strength this choice is impossible, but "with God all things are possible" *(Mark 10:27)*. This is why we are told to pray for those who have hurt us. In some cases, this person may have already died, but we can still pray for the ability to forgive him or her.

6. No question, forgiveness isn't always easy. The pain and the damage done to us can be devastating, leaving us hurt, crippled, broken. Healing will come, if we allow it, but holding on to bitterness and anger and resentment will make healing much harder, if possible at all.

7. The Cross is the best example of what it cost God Himself to forgive us. If the Lord can go through that for us, even though He knew that so many would, nevertheless, reject Him, then we certainly can learn to forgive, as well.

Finding Rest After Forgiveness = What happens next?

1. Joseph's family finally arrive in Egypt. There are no more dark secrets in the family. His brothers must have admitted to having sold Joseph when they explained to their father that the son he had thought had been killed was now prime minister of Egypt.

2. While it may not always be possible or wise to restore relationships, this does not mean that we cannot forgive. We may not be able to hug and weep with our offender, but we may want to voice our forgiveness either vocally or through a letter.

And then it is time to let go of pain to the utmost degree we can. Perhaps some pain will always remain, but at least we can be on the path to healing.

3. If the wound is deep, we will probably have to forgive many times. When memories of the wrong come to mind, we will need to go to God immediately in prayer and make the choice to forgive again.

4. Joseph firmly believed that his life was part of God's big plan to help save the then-known world from famine, and then to help his family fulfill God's promise to become a great nation. Knowing that God had overruled the evil plans of his brothers to bring about good helped Joseph to forgive.

Further Thought:

"As Joseph was sold to the heathen by his own brothers, so you may have been wounded by someone. Joseph was falsely accused and thrust into prison because of his virtue; so you may have gone through, not the same, but similar situation. Maybe despised and rejected because of who you are; and though guilty of no wrong, you were condemned upon the testimony of false witnesses. Notwithstanding, Joseph's patience and meekness under injustice and oppression, his ready forgiveness and noble benevolence toward his unnatural brothers, could represent yours now, that you are reading this book; an uncomplaining endurance of the malice and abuse of wicked men, and your forgiveness, of all who have come, or may not come to you confessing their wrongdoings and seeking pardon.

"Nothing can justify an unforgiving spirit. He who is unmerciful toward others shows that he himself is not a partaker of God's pardoning grace. In God's forgiveness the heart of the erring one is drawn close to the great heart of Infinite Love. The tide of divine compassion flows into the sinner's soul, and from him to the souls of others. The tenderness and mercy that Christ has revealed in His own precious life will be seen in those who become sharers of His grace." —Ellen G. White, *Christ's Object Lessons*, p. 251.

Wise Decisions Brings Victory At Last

The story end showing how, because he did not allow others and circumstances to discourage him, he was: Released from prison,became a prime minister in Egypt. Help to formulate a plan to saveEgypt during a time of famine. Had a chance for revenge against hisbad brothers, but did not. Get his family into a safe place in Egypt.

Let us go through your experience and see how this lesson canhelp you.

1. What is your family or environment background?
2. What decisions are you making for our life now, is it negatively being impacted by you past experience?
3. What people are saying to you and about you influencingyou negatively?
4. Do you allow people negative attacks on you to bother you?
5. Are you afraid of what people think or say about you?
6. Is it hard for you to forgive"?
7. Are you still carrying garbage because you refuse to forgive someone?
8. Are you a retaliating person?
9. Do you want to be able to look into the face of thosewho make themselves your enemies, and enjoy peace and calmness?
10. Are you willing to try the principles and advice of this book?
11. Make a list of your issues and how you will resolve them,
12. List some of your practices that have helped you, and that should have been included in this book.

- I wrote this on my Facebook page "I AM A HAPPY PERSON; I AM BLESSED

I am too blessed to worry about who likes me or who dislike me.
It is not about you, but all about me. I have more
important things to do.
If you love me, I love you; If you don't, I still love you.
If you support me, I support you; If you don't, I still support you.
If you hate me, I just don't care; I will never hate you, though,
I may hate your attitudes and actions.
I don't care; life goes on with or without you.
No one that tries to do me wrong is that good
or that important as to cause me to worry or get ulcers.

Your happiness is in the hands of God and in your hands. You decide whether you are going to let people torture you and make your life miserable, or you are going to be in control, and make yourown wise decisions.

Don't let others make you a stepping stone, instead, use the previous and current circumstance to be your stepping stone to success,a happier and better life for yourself.

REMEMBER, YOU MAKE THE DECISION, NOT OTHERS.

Chapter 11

Fighting Where the Fight Is Not

To enhance my book, I thought it would be a great idea to add a sermon my son Malcolm L Thomas preached. I like his slant, and it give a clear understanding also of the fight. Here goes:

We fight against our friends, classmates, church members, coworkers, and others, but the real enemy is Satan. He tricks us into fighting the wrong person. Other times the fight is within ourselves, as self is our biggest enemy.

To get you to fight where the fight is not, the enemy does several things. One of those things is that he deceives you about where the fight is.

Point 1 – The enemy wants you to think that you are in the right place.

June 4, 1940, Winston Churchill in perhaps his most famous speech, sent out a desperate plea for America to come and help England in the fight against Germany in World War 2.

"We shall fight on the beaches, we shall fight on the landing grounds, we shall fight in the fields and in the street, we shall fight in the hills; we shall never surrender, and even if, which I do not for a moment believe, this island or a large part of it were subjugated and starving, then our Empire beyond the seas, armed and guarded by the British fleet, would carry on the struggles, until, in God's good time, the new world, with all its power and might, steps forth to the rescue and the liberation of the old"

House of Commons 4 June 19400

So, eventually America decided to enter the war. There were a lot of things that happened to get America to that point, but that's not relevant to this story. The point is that America joined the war in December 1941. Shortly after that, the British and Americans decided for a major Allied invasion across the English Channel. The Allies were the countries that fought along with the British. The Axis fought alongside Germany.

By 1943, Adolf Hitler was aware of the threat of an invasion along France's northern coast. He put Erwin Rommel in charge of spearheading defense in the region.

The Americans were coming. (And the Canadians and Brits and Australians and New Zealanders) The Germans didn't know where, they didn't know when, but they knew they were coming. And to bring all that equipment and people, they knew the Americans had to come by sea.

So, the Germans knew the Americans were coming. The Americans knew that the Germans knew we were coming. What should the Americans do?

Matthew 24:43 But understand this:

> "If the owner of the house had known at what time of night the thief was coming, he would have kept watch and would not have let his house be broken into".

The Americans were coming. How important was this? The Americans arrived June 6, 1944. And by late August, all of Northern France had been liberated. And in 11 months and 2 days after landing at Normandy, the Germans would unconditionally surrender, and Hitler would be dead. That's how important it was.

In the months and weeks before D-Day, the Allies carried out a massive deception operation intended to make the Germans think the main invasion target was "pad-callay" Pas-de-Calais (the narrowest point between Britain and France) rather than Normandy. They also led the Germans to believe that Norway and other locations were also potential invasion targets.

How did they do that?

They used many tricks. They used double agents, fraudulent radio transmissions designed to be intercepted, and they let it be known that General George Patton (whom the Germans feared) would be leading an army based in England and land a Calais which was the closest point to England. Another trick they did was called "Seeing is Believing"

The Allies amassed a fake army called the First U.S. Army Group (FUSAG) commanded by Lt. General George Patton. When the

German spy planes made runs over Southeast England, they saw what looked like the buildup of a massive invasion force.

They saw tanks – balloons, vehicles, balloons, airplanes, painted wood, and amphibious landing craft. The German spy planes were convinced that there was a buildup of machines which only had to look realistic from a short distance, because pilots in an aircraft flying overhead could not tell the difference from far.

The deception worked so well, that even during the invasion, the Germans kept a large part of their forces in Calais still believing that Normandy was the decoy and that most of the soldiers and tanks were yet to land at Calais. After all, Calais was the port closest to England, the spies said that's where they were coming there. They intercepted radio traffic. The reconnaissance airplanes even saw General Patton's FUSAG troops amassed right across the English Channel from Calais. So the Germans waited at Calais.

On the 5th, the day the Allies were set to invade, a storm rolled in and raged along the entire French coast, including the English Channel. The weather was so bad that many of the Nazi's top military commanders, including Rommel, abandoned their posts to visit wives and mistresses in Germany and Paris. They thought there was no way the Allies could attempt an amphibious landing in such stormy seas. What the Germans didn't know was that Allied weather beacons had detected a break in the storm starting midnight on June 5 and continuing through June 6.

While the Germans were sleeping, the Americans were coming. And while the Germans were waiting at Calais, the Americans were coming at Normandy. Continuing their deception tactics, the Allies began their invasion by dropping hundreds of dummy paratroopers well inland of the eventual targets along the Normandy beaches.

This further convinced the Germans that these beaches were the deception, and that Calais was the real target. After all, it was the closest port to England. The Germans also kept a large contingency in Paris because they didn't want to lose control there. Then the Americans arrived at Utah Beach, Omaha Beach, Gold, Juno, and Sword.

Even as the Allies were invading in Normandy, the Germans remained convinced that Normandy was the decoy and the large FUSAG would be invading at Calais.

By the time the Germans realized that the Normandy landings where the actual offensive, Allied units were so well established in Normandy that they could not be dislodged. 156,000 American, British, and Canadian forces landed that day on those five beaches along a 50-mile stretch of France's Normandy region.

Within a week, over 326,000 troops, over 50,000 vehicles, and over 100,000 tons of equipment had landed at Normandy. Eventually, 2.5 million men and 500,000 vehicles would arrive through Normandy throughout the remainder of the war.

Even though the Germans knew the Americans were coming.

Point 1 – The enemy wants you to think that **you are in the right place**. …When you are not.

The Allies tricked Germany into putting their forces in the wrong place. They were looking for the enemy where the enemy wasn't. They were trying to fight where the fight wasn't.

Point 2 – The enemy wants you to think that **you are attacking the right person**.

When I was in 4th or maybe 5th grade, one of the kids in a grade below me wanted to fight. He may have been my age because I had skipped a grade. I don't remember what he wanted to fight me for. After school my classmates brought me a message from him. He was in the "forest" behind the school with a glass bottle waiting for me. I guess he broke the bottle so he could cut me.

What should I do?

Well, I don't go home through the forest. I walk or bike home from the front of the school. So, I didn't go the forest. In fact, I continued to play with my friends after school until it was time to go home, then I got on my bike and rode home the normal route. I didn't run from him, but I didn't stupidly go into the forest either. I could have gotten cut, we both could have gotten cut, or he alone may have gotten cut. We'll never know. But I knew it would go much better for me if I didn't go into the forest.

The next day I didn't avoid him in school, I didn't act afraid around him, I don't recall treating him significantly different. But after school he again waited for me in the forest…with the bottle. But that afternoon I still didn't go into the forest. That would be stupid. I am not stupid. Eventually he stopped waiting for me in the forest and we became friends again.

However…

He stopped trying to fight me, we got along and played together, and became friends again.

However, I lost a certain amount of respect for him, and he never got it back.

Who gets the most joy when people try to solve all their problems by fighting back instead of first seeking a peaceful Christian solution?

And who gets the most joy when people routinely try to resolve their problems by getting loud, getting passive-aggressive, bullying, by pressuring and by threatening to have their way?

Who gets the most joy when we fight the wrong enemy? If we could only see the metaphorical angel on people's shoulders urging them to do wrong, we would realize that people are pawns being used by the real enemy.

Point 2 – (repeat) – The enemy wants you to think that you are attacking the right person.

Peter chopped off the soldier's ear. James wanted to call down fire from heaven on the village for rejecting Jesus. And Saul's army though Goliath was the problem.

Peter didn't understand that Jesus was going willingly, that soldier wasn't strong enough to arrest the Creator. James didn't realize that this village must be able to freely choose to accept or reject Jesus because heaven is not forced upon us. And King Saul didn't realize that the real problem was not Goliath, but lack of faith and lack of having God on his side.

They all wanted to fight the wrong enemy.

Someone comes to you and says the wrong thing. And you put them in their place. You let them have it. You told them what was wrong with them—and their mama. But what did you accomplish?

A child hit you. A child teased you. A child got on your last nerve—again. And you finally gave them their comeuppance. Did you get the real enemy?

Now I know what you are thinking. Shouldn't I chastise the troublemakers and not the victims when the victims are simply responding to the troublemakers?

This sermon is not for the troublemakers. It is not directed at the people who have given themselves over to the devil's control, even unwittingly. Those people will always be here. And while they have yielded control to the devil, they will serve to tempt you, to try you, and to make you stronger by making you learn to rely on Jesus even more.

This sermon is for those of you who are still trying to be like Jesus. To be a peacemaker, to be merciful, to be meek. Those of you who still or wish to hunger and thirst after righteousness. Those of you are persecuted and called all manner of names falsely.

This sermon is to remind you or maybe inform you of who you are really fighting against.

Ephesians 6: 11 Put on the full armor of God, so that you can **take your stand against**

1. *That child that's always pushing you around.*
2. *That woman who is so cantankerous, you don't know how anyone can be her friend*

3. *That man that is always threatening everyone one, who insists on getting his way in everything*
4. *That spouse or ex-spouse who seems to treat everyone respectfully but you.*
5. *That boss who thinks they own you and gives you all the hard work and takes all your credit.*
6. *That church member who gossips about you and about everyone else and needs to be told off*

the devil's schemes. 12 For our struggle is not against flesh and blood,

Notice, it didn't say against "people". It says flesh and blood. Or we might interpret this as against ruler (politicians, presidents, kings), against authorities (judges, police, teachers, parents).

but against the **rulers**, against the **authorities**, against the **powers of this dark world** and against the **spiritual forces of evil in the heavenly realms.**

The Christian must contend with supernatural forces, but he is not to be left alone to engage in the conflict. The Saviour is the captain of his salvation, and with Him man may be more than conqueror. Faith and Works 92.3

We are fighting against Supernatural forces,

13 Therefore put on the full armor of God, so that when the day of evil comes, you may be able to stand your ground, and after you have done everything, to stand.

And that brings me to the last point I want to make.

Point 3 – The enemy wants you to think that you are able to win… on your own

You have a problem, you are able to use your smarts, your intelligence, or your quick wit to solve it. Now, you think you can solve anything. Therefore, you don't think you need to bring the Holy Spirit because you think you can do this on your own.

There are two stories in the Bible I want us to compare. Jonathan and Joshua.

The Israelites were fighting against the Philistines, as usual.

1 Samuel 14 (NIV): 6 Jonathan said to his young armor-bearer, "Come, let's go over to the outpost of those uncircumcised men. Perhaps the Lord will act in our behalf. Nothing can hinder the Lord from saving, whether by many or by few." 7 "Do all that you have in mind," his armor-bearer said. "Go ahead; I am with you heart and soul." 8 Jonathan said, "Come on, then; we will cross over toward them and let them see us. 9 If they say to us, 'Wait there until we come to you,' we will stay where we are and not go up to them. 10 But if they say, 'Come up to us,' we will climb up, because that will be our sign that the Lord has given them into our hands."

11 So both of them showed themselves to the Philistine outpost. "Look!" said the Philistines. "The Hebrews are crawling out of the holes they were hiding in." 12 The men of the outpost shouted to Jonathan and his armor-bearer, "Come up to us and we'll teach you a lesson." So Jonathan said to his armor-bearer, "Climb up after me; the Lord has given them into the hand of Israel." 13 Jonathan climbed up, using his hands and feet, with his armor-bearer right behind him. The Philistines fell before Jonathan, and his armor-bearer followed and killed behind

him. 14 In that first attack Jonathan and his armor-bearer killed some twenty men in an area of about half an acre.

But look how it ends.

15 Then panic struck the whole army—those in the camp and field, and those in the outposts and raiding parties—and the ground shook. It was a panic sent by God.

All Jonathan did was climb a hill. God did the rest. Well, that's a little misleading. Climbing the hill was one of the things that Jonathan did. The first was to go where he felt God leading. He didn't decide up front that God was going to bless his efforts. What he decided was, that if God wanted him to go forward, he would go forward. If it was not God's plan, then he would not go forward without God. And God punctuated his efforts by making the ground shake.

Now for Joshua going to fight against Ai.

A little background, Joshua had not yet attacked Jericho,

Joshua 5 (NKJ): 13 And it came to pass, when Joshua was by Jericho, that he lifted his eyes and looked, and behold, a Man stood opposite him with His sword drawn in His hand. And Joshua went to Him and said to Him, "Are You for us or for our adversaries?" 14 So He said, "No, but as Commander of the army of the Lord I have now come." And Joshua fell on his face to the earth and worshiped, and said to Him, "What does my Lord say to His servant?" 15 Then the Commander of the Lord's army said to Joshua, "Take your sandal off your foot, for the place where you stand is holy." And Joshua did so.

Joshua 6: 1 Now Jericho was securely shut up because of the children of Israel; none went out, and none came in. 2 And the Lord said to Joshua: "See! I have given Jericho into your hand, its king, and the mighty men of valor. 3 You shall march around the city... and Joshua received instructions from the Lord.

Soon after the fall of Jericho, Joshua determined to attack Ai, a small town among the ravines a few miles to the west of the Jordan

Valley. Spies sent to this place brought back the report that it was just a few inhabitants, and that they needed only a small force to overthrow it.

The great victory that God had gained for them [in Jericho] had made the Israelites self-confident. Because [God] had promised them the land of Canaan they felt secure, and failed to realize that divine help alone could give them success. Even Joshua laid his plans for the conquest of Ai without seeking counsel from God.

Before Jericho, Joshua asked, "What does my Lord say to His Servant?", but this time, he didn't ask God for help, for a sign, or for anything.

The Israelites had begun to exalt their own strength and to look with contempt upon their foes. An easy victory was expected, and they thought that three thousand men were enough to take the city.

Now, we know how the story ended. The Israelites were defeated by a smaller army.

Without God's leading, there would be no winning.

I said, "God's leading", I didn't say God's involvement. A lot of times, we are like Balaam. We try to do what we want, and then ask God to bless it. We should instead ask God for His will and be faithful to follow it.

Now Joshua was worried. Their enemies would not be afraid of them anymore. So, he threw himself on the ground and asked God, what now?

Joshua 7 (NIV): 10 The Lord said to Joshua, "Stand up! What are you doing down on your face? 11 Israel has sinned; they have violated my covenant, which I commanded them to keep. They have taken some of the devoted things; they have stolen, they have lied, they have put them with their own possessions. 12 **That is why the Israelites cannot stand against their enemies**; they turn their backs and run because they have been made liable to destruction. **I will not be with you anymore unless you destroy whatever among you is devoted to destruction**.

You see, they felt that Ai was the big enemy that <u>they</u> had to fight. But no, the battle was within themselves. The battle was to remain pure. The battle was to depend on God. We keep looking at other people as the problem, but the problem is too often within us.

When you see a person giving you a hard time. They are acting up, being bad, mistreating you. Open your eyes and see like Elisha where he could see all the angels surrounding their enemies even as his servant could not. Realize that the troublesome people in your life are there to prepare you for heaven. Whom the Lord loveth he chastiseth.

13 "Go, consecrate the people. Tell them, 'Consecrate yourselves in preparation for tomorrow; **for this is what the Lord, the God of Israel, says**: There are devoted things among you, Israel. **You cannot stand against your enemies until you remove them**.

Are we not winning because we are holding on to possessions, habits, attitudes, grudges, malice, or secret sins that prevent us from standing against our enemies? Things that prevent us from being right? Do we have things that prevent us from following God? Things that prevent us from having God be on our side? Or worse, things that keep us from being on God's side?

We keep viewing our adversaries as the enemy. We need to recognize them for what they are. They are a lesson for us. And the fight is often over self. And we can only win with God.

Chapter 12

Are you really Ready for the Fight?

The NLT version will be employed for this chapter..

Do you think you are ready for the fight? Do you really now understand the nature of the fight?

Satan playing chess with human

Before you answer, let me make something clear. Remember you are to:

"Put on all of God's armor so that you will be able to stand firm against all strategies of the devil. For <u>we are not fighting against flesh-and-blood enemies, but against evil rulers and authorities of the unseen world, against mighty powers in this dark world, and against evil spirits in the heavenly places.</u> Therefore, put on every piece of God's armor so you will be able to resist the enemy in the time of evil. Then after the battle you will still be standing firm" Ephesians 6:11-13 NLT

God found it necessary to put on His amour while fighting the enemy.

"He was amazed to see that no one intervened to help the oppressed. So he himself stepped in to save them with his strong arm, and his justice sustained him. <u>He put on righteousness as his body armor and placed the helmet of salvation on his head.</u> He clothed himself with a robe of vengeance and wrapped himself in a cloak of divine passion. He will repay his enemies for their evil deeds. His fury will fall on his foes. He will pay them back even to the ends of the earth". Isaiah 59:16-18 NLT

To fully understand the parameters of our fight, as human beings, let me explain: We were programmed by God from the beginning to have certain potential. This programming does not affect of power of choice. We were giving the power of choice to exercise those potentials and be happy and successful or deviate from them and bring unhappiness to ourselves and others.

"God, the creator, (Genesis:1 2); determined what He wanted to make man (Genesis 1 and 2; with what material he wanted to use (dust of the ground. Gen. 2:7; and for what purpose to bring glory to Him, and to have dominion over the earth. John 17:4; Eccles 12:13"

Based on what is stated above, I repeat

1. In the beginning, God created…man,"
2. God formed man out of the dust of the ground
3. He said let us make man in our image after our likeness
4. He said let them glorify me, be fruitful and have dominion over all things on earth.

The complication, problem, or perhaps what occurs at times I should say, is that one may misuse the thing created for the wrong purpose. Seeking its own purpose instead of the creator's intended one. Man, because of the choice given to him, can do that which God, nor nature, had not intended for him to do. That is, go outside of what is natural or what the creator intended it to be because of some inner urge to satisfy his ego..

God's purpose for us is predetermined and comes with an instruction manual (the Bible)"

Wow, that is powerful. Did you get the impact? This should change your life for good, and make it enjoyable, even as you face challenges. It should improve your personal relationship. People and circumstance should not bother you; you should have a better attitude towards them.

The Garden Of Eden...Paradise

Even at the sound of being repetitious, I want to emphasize that, when God made man (and He had you and me in mind), it was His plan that man would glorify him. Before God formed man, He set up a blueprint for his life. Following this blueprint in constructing his life, every human would bring the best results in their lives. The master Architect says:

> I will say to the north and south,
> 'Bring my sons and daughters back to Israel
> from the distant corners of the earth.
> Bring all who claim me as their God,
> for ***I have made them for my glory.***
> It was I who created them.'" Isa. 43:6-7 NLT

"what are mere mortals that you should think about them, human beings that you should care for them? Yet you made them only a little lower than God and crowned them with glory and honor. You gave them charge of everything you made, putting all things under their authority—" Psalm 8:4-6 NLT

At the beginning of each life is the potential for success and happiness, if, in the construction of one's life, the Bible outlined blueprint is followed.

The problem is, men, instead of following the blueprint, they make so many inventions with the material, the form and lifestyle God use to make them and presented to them in God's blueprint; they have invented their own choosing

"God created people to be virtuous, but they have each turned to follow their own downward path." Ecclesiastes 7:29 NLT

Due to the entrance of sin and the separation from God, the earth and living have become difficult, traumatic, problematic, etc. What we are experiencing today, and the attitude of many people was not what God intended for us upon this earth. There is also the evil forces that humans would have to contend with;, powers far beyond human capacity to fight them off, therefore God, before we were created or born, set out for us some guidelines though His manual, the Bible, for living for us on this earth; how to live on this earth, how to contend with these evil forces and their puppets in human forms, and prepare us for a renewed earth and conditions.

From the very beginning God has placed in us the ability to make choices; he has not placed in us the potential to direct our own lives, but to choose who we would allow to direct us--God or the devil--. Jeremiah confirms this when he said in his prayer: "

"I know, LORD, that our lives are not our own. We are not able to plan our own course" Jeremiah 10:23 MLT.

So, we can choose God to direct us to realize our God-given potential to do good or we can choose Satan to direct us to make evil and wrong choices.

Very often we hear people say, "I am my own man or woman, I make my own choices." Wrong. Go out into a pasture with tall grasses and a high wind. Look at how they seems to be doing their own thing, enjoying themselves. But are they really doing it on the own volition, No, the wind is dictating their pace. So is it with many of us. The evil one is using us as puppets, and we do not even realize it. God' s guideline recommends that you:

"Seek his will in all you do, and he will show you which path to take" Proverb 3:16.

The evil one wants to defeat this purpose, fight us; set our family, friends, and even church members against us. But God. knowing this, has placed into us from the beginning, the potential for overcoming and be successful. Let us look at nature. Nature follows the guidelines of God faithfully, and groans for a renovation of the earth.

In the family movie "The Ugly Dachshund" This Great Dane was place in the company of dachshunds, and eventually began to act and crawl on the ground like them. Until he saw a female Great Dane and a picture of what a Great Dane looks like, that he stood up erect like a real Great Dane. Many Christians and also non-Christians today are acting like human dachshunds when God Made us to be human Great Danes.

In any seed are the potential for what God wanted it to become. Each type of seed has its own potential. The size, color, savor, directing to grow toward, amount, and so forth. An apple seed has the potential for apples and not oranges. The palm tree seed has the potential of growing tall into the air, and not grow underground like the potatoes. Some seeds do not bear fruit, but just gives shade or decoration. In like manner, each of us is born and started out with our own purpose and individuality. People don't make us or make us do things. We hear some people often say, "She or he made me do it" No, you made that choice. But what happens, many try to assume the potential of others, which they do not have. They try to make their own lifestyle; they try to cultivate their own way of being, and this messes up their lives. Therefore, so many are not happy, and eventually they are in such disarray.

You might have heard the story of the eagle egg that was hatched by a chicken. When the eagle was born it acted and did everything like a chicken, it barely flew off the ground or spread its wings. Until one day, someone saw the eagle in it and the potential God placed in eagle before creation.

It was taken to a hill where the sun was shining. The man threw it into the air saying "You are not a chicken you are and eagle, so fly like an eagle"

This was not successful, for each time it flutters on the ground. Until, after several attempts, the man said to it again: "You are not a chicken, you are and eagle, so fly like an eagle"

This time, this eagle. warmth by the heath of the sun, refreshes by the winds, feeling a freedom in the open sky, began to fulfill its God's given ability and potentials, opened up and extended its wings, (and what length, what beauty what majesty), he flew into the blue sky, following the manual God gave it, and disappeared into the heavens.

God's original plan for us was to be soaring eagles not fluttering chickens. But we often act like chickens. There is concrete evidences that God made in us the ability to love and forgive others, but instead, we choose to hate and boast about our unforgiving spirit; we choose to fight when God said to reconcile; we choose to be selfish when God placed into us an unselfish manner; we chose to noirish our temper while God placed into us patience. The choice of action is and has always been with us from the beginning, but we make wrong and selfish choices

In the case of Alejandro, in chapter three "Let's Get Ready To Rumble", he chose to respond positively with the milk thrown on him incident, instead of cursing or retaliating. Roy in chapter six "Are You A Church?" who said that he was a church, chose to behave how God intended him to behave while representing God on this earth, from his birth. Rose, in chapter seven "You Can Only Give What You Have" chose to give good, lovely, beautiful fruits, instead of seeking revenge. Jesus set for us the example of potentials, choices, and lifestyle, to show us how to do it, and to offers His lifestyle it to us freely. There is a text that in summary say, if you chose to gain your life by your own actions and not by those outlines in the Bible and by God from the beginning for you, you will lose it. But if you lose it here, now upon this earth by following his outline, you will find it and eternally have it. Remember, this world is not our final resting and happiness zone. Therefore, be ready for the fight has God outlined for you and is training you how to fight.

God gave you, my dear reader, the power of choice. How will you choose to fight, still your way or God's way? The choice is always yours. God says to you, right now:

"The LORD your God will change your heart[and the hearts of all your descendants, so that you will love him with all your heart and soul and so you may live! The LORD your God will inflict all these curses on your enemies and on those who hate and persecute you. Then you will again obey the LORD and keep all his commands that I am giving you today.

"The LORD your God will then make you successful in everything you do. He will give you many children and numerous livestock, and he will cause your fields to produce abundant harvests, for the LORD will again delight in being good to you as he was to your ancestors. The LORD your God will delight in you if you obey his voice and keep the commands and decrees written in this Book of Instruction, and if you turn to the LORD your God with all your heart and soul.

The Choice of Life or Death

"This command I am giving you today is not too difficult for you, and it is not beyond your reach. It is not kept in heaven, so distant that you must ask, 'Who will go up to heaven and bring it down so we can hear it and obey?' It is not kept beyond the sea, so far away that you must ask, 'Who will cross the sea to bring it to us so we can hear it and obey?' No, the message is very close at hand; it is on your lips and in your heart so that you can obey it.

"Now listen! Today I am giving you a choice between life and death, between prosperity and disaster. For I command you this day to love the LORD your God and to keep his commands, decrees, and regulations by walking in his ways. If you do this, you will live and multiply, and the LORD your God will bless you and the land you are about to enter and occupy.

"But if your heart turns away and you refuse to listen, and if you are drawn away to serve and worship other gods, then I warn you now that you will certainly be destroyed. You will not live a long, good life in the land you are crossing the Jordan to occupy.

"Today I have given you the choice between life and death, between blessings and curses. Now I call on heaven and earth to witness the choice you make. Oh, that you would choose life, so that you and your descendants might live! Deut. 30:6-18 LVT

May your answer now and forever be: Lord, I come to you; Let my heart be changed Author: **Geoff Bullock**

Lord, I come to you

Let my heart be changed, renewed.

Flowing from the grace

That I found in you.

Lord. I have come to know

The weakness I see in me

Will be stripped away

By the power of your love.

Hold me close

Let your love surround me

Bring me near

Draw me to your side.

And as I wait

I'll rise up like an eagle

And I will soar with you

Your spirit leads me on

In the power of your love.

Lord, unveil my eyes

Let me see you face to face

The knowledge of your love

As you live in me.

Lord renew my mind

As Your will unfolds in my life

In living every day

By the power of your love.

Don't stop now, the best chapter is yet to come.

Chapter 13

The Knockout

Come, Learn of Me

Thr**T**his is what every boxer aims to achieve: a knockout is a blow that would end the fight and put the opponent outof commission. For our "God fight," we cannot learn this one from boxing. We must learn it from the greatest spiritual boxerever lived.

> Wherefore seeing we also are compassed about with so great a cloud of witnesses, let us lay aside every weight, and the sin which doth so easilybeset us, and let us run with patience the race that is set before us, *Looking unto Jesus the authorand finisher of our faith; who for the joy that was set before him endured the cross, despising the shame,*and is set down at the right hand of the throne ofGod. (Heb. 12:1–2; italic mine)

"Oi, you! You're causing upset bearing that cross in public!"

Here is the scenario.

Jesus was about to fulfill the last part of his goal: to lay downHis life for His people and had just finished praying to His Father and explaining to His Father the agony He felt. He was then willing to go through it when a group of Roman soldiers came to arrest Him.

> Then they came and laid hands on Jesus and took Him. And suddenly, one of those (Peter) *who were* with Jesus stretched out *his* hand and drew his sword, struck the servant of the high priest, and cut off his ear. But Jesus said to him, "Put your sword in its place, for all who take the sword will perish by the sword. Or do you think that I cannot now pray to My Father, and He will provide Me with more than twelve legions of angels? How then could the Scriptures be fulfilled, that it must happen thus?" (Matt. 26:50–54, NKJV)

"But Jesus answered and said, 'Permit even this.' And He touched His ear and healed Him" (Luke 22:51).

When the soldiers were about to take Jesus, Peter started a *bad fight*. He cut off the ear of a soldier. Jesus told him that if he lives by the sword, he would die by the sword. Then Jesus showed him the *good fight*. He restored the ear back.

Physical and unhealthy retaliation will not solve the problem nor will back and forth revenging. The Christian have a unique way to get revenge. The knockout is the ultimate blow. It is intended to be final. Muhammad Ali is said to be the greatest boxer of all time. I beg to differ. The greatest boxer and undisputed champion of the universe is Jesus Himself. This is what He said, "Jesus said, 'My kingdom is not of this world. If it were, my servants would fight to prevent my arrest by the Jewish leaders. But now my kingdom is from another place.'" (John 18:36).

And this is what was said of Him, "When they hurled their insults at him, he did not retaliate; when he suffered, he made no threats. Instead, he entrusted himself to him who judges justly" (1 Peter 2:23).

Was He by not defending himself or retaliating, a weakling? Absolutely not. Here is why: He had a goal set for himself, and nothing was going to deter him from achieving it.

The Goal

1. For the Son of Man came to seek and to save the lost (Luke 19:10).[4]

2. And (when He was a child) He said to them, "Why did you seek Me? Did you not know that I must be about My Father's business?" (Luke 2:49).

3. Jesus said to them, "My food is to do the will of Him whosent Me, and to finish His work" (John 4:34).[5]

4. For I have come down from heaven, not to do My own will, but the will of Him who sent Me. (John 6:37–39).

4.

---

[4] https://www.biblegateway.com/passage/?search=Luke+19:10&version=NIV.

[5] https://www.biblegateway.com/passage/?search=John+4:34&version=NKJV.

He set the example for us to follow.

1. Learn of Him.
2. Set your goals.
3. Analyze situation before you act.
4. Recycle if needed or possible.
5. Remember that you are in control, not the other person or circumstances,
6. Build your arsenal. You cannot give what you don't have.
7. Follow the guidelines Christ has given us.
8. Remember, you are more than a conquers through the strength God gives you.
9. Go, win your battles and wars.

Conclusion

Y ou may ask: what does all this have to do with me? I am gladyou ask. Here, let me remind you of what it has to do with you.

A. The Bible says that there are two spiritual kingdoms in this universe waring against each other: One is evil and fights dirty, headed by Satan himself. The other is the one who fights the good fight headed by Jesus.

B. As humans, our goal is not to live too comfortably with the existing conditions of our world today but be on our journey to the country Jesus had intended for us from thebeginning.

C. We cannot outsmart nor outpunch the evil one. He uses people as puppets to get at us. He uses circumstances to defeat us.

D. He is a defeated foe, and Jesus knows how to defeat him. Christ has always been successful against him. So Jesus gave us methods to defeat him. These methods may look silly or foolish to us, but they are proven to succeed.

E. If we ignore these methods and use our own, we may *apparently* succeed here but finally lose the ultimate, priceless, and eternal goal. When we realize our mistake, it would then be too late. We would then say like the man on the plane in the commercial, "I could have had a V8."

F. It is a matter of choice for us.

The counsel then is found in Ephesians 6:10–18, New King James Version (NKJV).

ARMOR OF GOD

Eph 6:14–17

The Whole Armor of God

Finally, my brethren, be strong in the Lord and in the power of His might. Put on the whole armor of God, that you may be able to stand against the wiles of the devil. For we do not wrestle against flesh and blood, but against principalities, against powers, against the rulers of the darkness of this age, against spiritual *hosts* of wickedness in the heavenly *places*. Therefore, take up the whole armor of God, that you may be able to withstand in the evil day, and having done all, to stand.

Stand therefore, having girded your waist with truth, having put on the breastplate of righteousness, and having shod your feet with the preparation of the gospel of peace; above all, taking the shield of faith with which you will be able to quench all the fiery darts of the wicked one. And take the helmet of salvation, and the sword of the Spirit, which is the word of God; praying always with all prayer and supplication in the Spirit, being watchful to this end with all perseverance and supplication for all the saints.[6]

Does this work? Yes, it does. I am living proof. When I tell some people my experiences, they do not believe me and think I am lying. You see, not because you did not or cannot experience something it means that it is not possible. Don't measure someone's by your yardstick.

I personally have developed and used these skills perfectly. No one can annoy me, to the extent, where it causes me to react against them. Do I feel something when I face these challenges? Yes, I feel it and want to retaliate, but since I am in control, I manage my reaction. I follow the instructions I am giving you in this book, and, *bingo*, I succeed.

Take it from me. It worked for Christ, and it works for me. When you go to the doctor and he prescribes your medication, it may not look good or taste good to you. But he is your doctor. He has the experience and knows what is good for you. But no matter how good and effective the medication may be, it would be useless to you if you do not take it. Please take it. You will be and feel better. "Most assuredly, I say to you, a servant is not greater than his master; nor is he who is sent greater than he who sent him. If you know these things, blessed are you if you do them" (John 13:16–18).

In conclusion, I leave you the advice from the Apostle Paul in Romans 12 (NKJV).

Living Sacrifices to God

I beseech you therefore, brethren, by the mercies of God, that you present your bodies a living sacrifice, holy, acceptable to God, *which is* your reasonable service. And do not be conformed to this world, but be transformed by the renewing of your mind, that you may prove what *is* that good and acceptable and perfect will of God.

---

[6] https://www.biblegateway.com/passage/?search=Eph.+6%3A10-18&version=NKJV#fen-NKJV-29350a.

For I say, through the grace given to me, to everyone who is among you, not to think *of himself* more highly than he ought to think, but to think soberly, as God has dealt to each one a measure of faith.

Behave Like a Christian

Let love *be* without hypocrisy. Abhor what is evil. Cling to what is good. *Be* kindly affectionate to one another with brotherly love, in honor giving preference to one another; not lagging in diligence, fervent in spirit, serving the Lord; rejoicing in hope, patient in tribulation, continuing steadfastly in prayer; distributing to the needs of the saints, given to hospitality.

Bless those who persecute you; bless and do not curse. Rejoice with those who rejoice, and weep with those who weep. Be of the same mind toward one another. Do not set your mind on high things, but associate with the humble. Do not be wise in your own opinion.

Repay no one evil for evil. Have regard for good things in the sight of all men. If it is possible, as much as depends on you, live peaceably with all men. Beloved, do not avenge yourselves, but *rather* give place to wrath; for it is written, "Vengeance *is* Mine, I will repay," says the Lord. Therefore, "If your enemy is hungry, feed him; If he is thirsty, give him a drink; For in so doing you will heap coals of fire on his head."

Do not be overcome by evil but overcome evil with good. (Rom. 12:9–21)

Please send your comments on this book to my publishers. If you have any story, experience, or comments that would enhance it, kindly let me know at hetp41141@gmail.com. You may be also helping other. And by the way, indicate if you give permission to include it in another publishing. Thank you.

Coming soon:

1. Want to Hear Stories about and from Grandpa?
2. Lemons that Cannot Make Lemonade
3. The GOAT Love Story
4. God and I choose Life

About the Author

Hubert E. Thomas was born in Colon, Republic of Panama. His elementary studies was at Escuela República de Bolivia, Colon, Panama. His high school was at Colegio Abel Bravo, Colon, Panama. He received a AA ministerial degree at Colegio Vocacional de América Central, Alajuela, Costa Rica. His bachelor's degree was at West Indies College, Mandeville, Jamaica (graduated as class president). His master's degree was from Andrews University, Berrien Springs, Michigan. After graduation, he served as a pastor of a six-church bilingual district in the Panama conference. He was a pastor and treasurer in Cayman Islands, Mission of Seventh day Adventists. He was assigned Accounts receivable at the Andrews Memorial Hospital in Jamaica. He served as a pastor of the Spanish churches and internal auditor for North Caribbean Conference (St. Croix). He was an internal auditor for Inter-American Division of Seventh-Day Adventists (FL) and at the writing of this book, an internal Auditor for South Atlantic Conference of Seventh-day Adventists. He was a Special Education school bus driver for Montgomery (MD) and Gwinnett Counties (GA).

www.ingramcontent.com/pod-product-compliance
Lightning Source LLC
Chambersburg PA
CBHW040903120626
46551CB00006B/630